Diet recommendations for Kidney stones

Please check these recommendations always with a nutrition consultant, therapist, doctor or dietician. The recipes and the list of ingredients are supporting the conventional medical therapy. The calorie disclosures of fresh ingredients (fruit and vegetables) vary according to quality and time of harvest. The contents were checked by a dietician and a nutrition consultant for the Traditional Chinese Medicine (TCM).

Author:
©2017 Josef Miligui
www.ebns.at

Source:
The lists are created from the EBNS database for nutritional counseling. The database is used by dietitians, therapists and doctors for advising the patient / client.

Literature:
The specialist literature and the training documents of the German and Austrian dietary and traditional Chinese medicine serve as a knowledge base. We have used the documents as a basis of knowledge, adapted it to our experience and completed them.
http://di-book.com

Title Photo:
©2008 Erika Weixlbaumer

Production and publishing:
BoD – Books on Demand, Norderstedt
ISBN 9783746025926

Diet recommendations for DIETETICS - Protein and electrolyte - kidney - Kidney stones (nephrolithiasis)

1 Treatment strategy

The basis of nutritional therapy is an ovo-lacto-vegetabile diet - ie. Vegetable foods are preferable to the animal: cereals, beans, vegetables, nuts and fruits.
Important is the adequate supply of liquid and the consumption of calcium-rich foods.
Phosphate, purine or oxalic acid foods should be avoided according to kidney stone type.
Drinks recommended: clear water, fruit and herbal teas, diluted fruit juices, mineral water with high
magnesium content and little sodium.

2 Avoid

Large amounts of protein and fat (especially animal fat), spinach, rhubarb, offal, processed cheese, cola, peanuts, cocoa and chocolate as well as black and green tea. Bean coffee and alcohol.

3 Breakfast

kkal. per serving
Barley and vegetable soup 281
Barley mash with berries 112
Barley mash with plums 106
Barley mash with steamed pear 113

4 Snack

5 Lunch

6 Afternoon

7 Dinner

8 Any time

9 Recipes

(recommendable) = You can use more.
(little) = You should use less than specified or omit.

9.1 Artichoke soup

Detoxifying, supports urination, regulates digestion, stimulates appetite, gentle laxative, forcing spleen, promotes weight loss. Strengthens gastrointestinal function, expands blood vessels, prevents cancer.

Cooking time approx. 40 min
Calories p. portion: 142
3 portions
Allergens: GLN

Quantity of ingredients:
Sesame, white 1 teaspoon / 10g. (yes)
Butter Bio 1 table spoon / 20g. (little)
Onion (shallot) 1 piece / 20g. (yes)
Lemon 1/4 piece / 8g. (yes)
Salt 1 pinch / 0,5g. (little)
Sesame paste (Tahini) 1 table spoon / 10g. (yes)
Nutmeg 1 pinch / 0,5g. (yes)
Corn flour 1 table spoon / 10g. (yes)
Artichoke 4 pieces / 400g. (yes)
Lemon peel 1/4 piece / g. (yes)
Turmeric (yellow root) 1 pinch / 1g. (yes)
Basic recipe for a vegetable soup (nutritious) 1 cup / 250g. (yes)

Cooking instructions:
Boil the artichokes in 2 liters of water with salt until the outer leaves are light removable. Remove leaves and flower center (fibrous) so that only the soil remains.
Melt the butter, cut the onion into small pieces and steam gently; add some cornmeal, nutmeg; brew with vegetable soup; add salt, a little lemon peel and juice, turmeric and artichoke bottoms, cook gently and puree; Season with Tahin and sprinkle with sesame before serving.

9.2 Asparagus and herb ragout

Diuretic, improves blood circulation, prevents cancer, dissolves stagnation, promotes weight loss. Good to fight immunodeficiency, loss of appetite, flatulence, high blood pressure, depressions, diabetes, diarrhea, stimulates liver function.
Cooking time approx. 30 min
Calories p. portion: 168
4 portions
Allergens: GL

Quantity of ingredients:
Coriander 1/4 teaspoon / 1g. (yes)
Lemon juice 1 teaspoon / 3g. (yes)
Lemon peel 1/2 piece / 3g. (yes)
Asparagus (green or white) 1,8 lbs / 800g. (yes)
Parsley 1 Bunch / 125g. (yes)
Potato 7/8 lbs / 400g. (yes)
Crème fraiche cheese 2 table spoons / 30g. (little)
Nutmeg 1 pinch / 0,3g. (yes)
Basic recipe for a vegetable soup (nutritious) 2 cups / 500g. (yes)

Cooking instructions:
Cook potatoes with plenty of salted water about 20 min. until soft.
Heat the vegetable stock with lemon zest, coriander and nutmeg till it boil. Cook the peeled and sliced asparagus in it.
Drain asparagus in a sieve. Collect the cooking liquid.
In the blender mix 200 g of cooked asparagus (the lower ends), cooking liquid and parsley to a smooth sauce. Beat the sauce with crème fraiche until smooth. Add asparagus and heat again and season with lemon juice, salt and pepper. Serve with the potatoes.

9.3 Barley and vegetable soup

Supports urination, detoxifying, promotes spleen and liver, reduces blood pressure, strengthens immune system, prevents cancer, reduces radiation damage, promotes digestion, helps to digest fat, harmonizes
Cooking time approx. 2 hours
Calories p. portion: 281
3 portions
Allergens: AGL

Quantity of ingredients:
Tomato 1 piece / 50g. (yes)
Pepper (ground) 1 pinch / 0,5g. (yes)
Parsley 1 teaspoon / 3g. (yes)
Celery sticks 2 branches / 20g. (yes)
Onion (shallot) 1 piece / 20g. (yes)
Cumin (Caraway seed) 1 knife tip / 0,5g. (yes)
Sunflower oil 1 table spoon / 10g. (yes)
Peas, green 5/8 lbs - 8oz / 250g. (yes)
Carrot 2 pieces / 150g. (yes)
Salt 1 pinch / 1g. (little)
Water 1 cup / 250g. (yes)
Shiitake, dried 1/8 oz / 4g. (yes)
Butter Bio 1 teaspoon / 3g. (little)
French beans Handful / 30g. (little)
Barley 1 cup / 120g. (yes)

Cooking instructions:
Soak the barley in the evening for the next day. Soak the mushrooms separately at the next day. Brown onion and cumin in oil, then boil with water. Add the chopped vegetables, some salt, the barley and the shiitake mushrooms and cook everything to a thick soup. At the end, season with pepper, parsley and a little butter.

9.4   Barley mash with berries

Diuretic, forcing spleen, supports urination, laxative, promotes digestion, detoxifying, promotes perspiration, dissolves stagnation.
Cooking time approx. 2 hours
Calories p. portion: 113
5 portions
Allergens: A

Quantity of ingredients:
Water 10 cups / 1200g. (yes)
Barley malt 1 table spoon / 15g. (yes)
Cocoa 1 pinch / 1g. (little)
Barley 1 cup / 120g. (yes)
Salt 1 pinch / 1g. (little)
Cardamom 3 capsules / 1g. (yes)
Ginger fresh 2 slices / 2g. (yes)
Lemon Balm (fresh) 2-4 leaves / 3g. (yes)
Raspberry 5/8 lbs - 8oz / 250g. (yes)

Cooking instructions:
Boil the barley with water, ginger and cardamom pods in a large saucepan. Close pot with a lid and cook over low heat for about 2 hours.
For 2 servings of cooked barley porridge, place about 2 ladles in a bowl. Stir with sunflower seeds, malt, cocoa powder and a pinch of salt. Stir fresh berries into the porridge and serve sprinkled with fresh mint or lemon balm.
Tip: The pre-cooked barley porridge (without fruit) can be stored well in the refrigerator and used for sweet or savory dishes, e.g. with stewed vegetables or fruit seasoned compote.

9.5 Barley mash with plums

Promotes spleen, diuretic, forcing spleen, supports urination, relaxes, reduces internal heat.
Cooking time approx. 25 min
Calories p. portion: 107
5 portions
Allergens: AG

Quantity of ingredients:
Water 10 cups / 1200g. (yes)
Butter Bio 2 teaspoons / 6g. (little)
Sugar cane sugar 1/2 teaspoon / 2g. (yes)
Plum 1 cup / 120g. (yes)
Barley 1 cup / 120g. (yes)

Cooking instructions:
Grind coarse the barley and roast it dry. Add hot water, add ginger and cardamom and let it swell to a pulp in low heat. Core the plums and boil for 10 minutes with a little water. At the end, add the stewed plums, a little butter and sweetener.
Variant: If you want to go fast, you can use barley flakes instead of shot.

9.6 Barley mash with steamed pear

Promotes digestion, supports urination, promotes spleen, diuretic, forcing spleen, relaxes, promotes perspiration.
Cooking time approx. 25 min
Calories p. portion: 114
5 portions
Allergens: A

Quantity of ingredients:
Salt 1 pinch / 1g. (little)
Cardamom 3 capsules / 1g. (yes)
Ginger fresh 2 slices / 2g. (yes)
Pear 1 piece / 200g. (yes)
Barley 1 cup / 120g. (yes)
Sugar cane sugar 1/2 teaspoon / 5g. (yes)
Water 10 cups / 1200g. (yes)

Cooking instructions:
Grind coarse the barley and roast it dry. Add hot water, add ginger and cardamom and let it swell to a pulp in low heat. Peel and dice the pear and boil for 10 minutes with a little water. At the end, add the stewed pear, a little butter and sweetener.

Variant: If you want to go fast, you can use barley flakes instead of shot.

9.7 Barley soup

Diuretic, forcing spleen, supports urination, stimulates liver function, antioxidativ, promotes digestion, detoxifying, reduces blood lipids, stimulates, dissolves stagnation.
Cooking time approx. 25 min
Calories p. portion: 265
2 portions
Allergens: A

Quantity of ingredients:
Salt 1 pinch / 1g. (little)
Water 1 1/2 cups / 240g. (yes)
Olive oil 1 table spoon / 10g. (yes)
Barley 1 cup / 120g. (yes)
Ginger fresh 1/2 teaspoon / 1g. (yes)
Parsley 2 table spoons / 30g. (yes)

Cooking instructions:
Roast the barley in the pan, then grind it to the ground, and boil with water, some salt and ginger to a mash. Before serving add oil and parsley.

Variant: You can add a better taste to the dish if you cook it with prepared vegetable or meat broth.

9.8 Basic recipe for a reissue soup (Congee)

Low fat content, for the drainage of the body overweight and high blood pressure.
Cooking time approx. 2-4 hours
Calories p. portion: 140
3 portions
Allergens:

Quantity of ingredients:
Rice variety any 1 cup / 120g. (yes)
Water 6 cups / 700g. (yes)

Cooking instructions:
Cook rice and water in a ratio of about 1: 6. The amount of water determines the thickness of the mash (matter of taste).
Put the rice in a saucepan with a heavy lid. It is important to simmer the rice after a short boil on the slightest flame, otherwise it burns.
Boil the rice for 2-4 hours. The longer he cooks, the more he strengthens.
If you want to eat the dish for breakfast, you can put the rice on just before bedtime.
To be on the safe side, you should first check the behavior of your pot and cooker under observation for a similar amount of time, so that nothing burns.
Refrigerate for later use.

9.9 Basic recipe for a vegetable soup, nutritious

Reduces blood pressure, strengthens immune system, prevents cancer, forcing spleen, dissolves stagnation, promotes weight loss. Good to fight immunodeficiency, high blood pressure, depressions, diabetes, diarrhea, reduces blood lipids.
Cooking time approx. 2-3 hours
Calories p. portion: 48
5 portions
Allergens: L

Quantity of ingredients:
Olive oil 1 table spoon / 4g. (yes)
Parsnip 3/8 lbs - 6oz / 150g. (yes)
Thyme dried 1 pinch / 1g. (yes)
Lovage 1 table spoon / 3g. (yes)
Bay leaf 2 leaves / 1g. (yes)

Carrot 3 pieces / 200g. (yes)
Onion white 1 piece / 60g. (yes)
Juniper berry 6 pieces / 6g. (yes)
Salt 1 pinch / 1g. (little)
Lemon 1/2 piece / 25g. (yes)
Celery root 1 cup / 100g. (yes)
Ginger fresh 1/2 teaspoon / 2g. (yes)
Water 3 cups / 650g. (yes)

Cooking instructions:
Cut the vegetables into cubes.
Heat oil in hot pot, fry shortly onions and vegetables.
Add cold water, then add ginger, bay leaf and lemon juice.
Season with juniper, thyme and lovage. Cover for 2 - 3 hours on a low
heat and simmer.
The used vegetables should be thrown away.
The basic recipe serves as a soup base and to refine vegetables,
legumes or cereals.
If you want to eat vegetable soup immediately, add the desired
vegetables half an hour before.
Refrigerate for later use.

9.10 Basmati rice + Zucchini tofu dish

Diuretic, supports urination, harmonizes spleen and stomach, reduces
flatulence, good to fight body overweight and high blood pressure.
Antioxidativ, promotes digestion, perspiration, reduces blood lipids,
forcing spleen.
Cooking time approx. 20 min
Calories p. portion: 146
4 portions
Allergens: E

Quantity of ingredients:
Rice Basmati 1/2 cup / 60g. (yes)
Coriander 1/2 teaspoon / 4g. (yes)
Olive oil 2 table spoons / 6g. (yes)
Soy Tofu 5/8 lbs - 8oz / 250g. (little)
Water 3 cups / 200g. (yes)
Zucchini 1 piece / 700g. (yes)
Ginger fresh 1/2 teaspoon / 4g. (yes)

Cooking instructions:
Cut tofu cubes and marinate with olive oil, tamari, crushed coriander and ginger. Leave at least 1 hour.
Cook Basmati rice with the water. You can season with onion and cardamom.
Roast zucchini and tofu in pan in the hot oil for approx. 5-7 min.
Serve rice and tofu on a plate.
Add the parsley.
Can also be used as a salad for the home and on the go.

9.11 Black root with yogurt

Stimulates kidney, bladder and forces the cleaning of the body. In the physiological sense, they generally stimulate the glands in the organism. Good to fight acute or chronic constipation of the intestine. Rich in Vitamins and trace elements.
Cooking time approx. 20 min
Calories p. portion: 424
2 portions
Allergens: AG

Quantity of ingredients:
Yogurt (natural, 1.5% fat) 4 table spoons / 80g. (yes)
Salt 1 pinch / 1g. (little)
Salsify 1 lbs / 400g. (yes)
Herbs various 1 table spoon / 8g. (yes)
Herbs various 2 table spoons / 6g. (yes)
Multi-grain bread (gray bread) 6 slices / 120g. (yes)

Cooking instructions:
Peel the salsify and simmer in salted water until tender. Pour away the water, cool the salsify and cut it to size.
Cover with yoghurt and sprinkle with fresh herbs. Serve with the bread.
You can also use the salsify from the conserve.

9.12 Boiled celery salad with exotic spices

Forcing spleen, relieves diarrhea, antibacterial, blood-forming, blood detoxifying, reduces inflammation, diuretic, improves blood circulation.
Cooking time approx. 30 min
Calories p. portion: 166
4 portions
Allergens: GLMNO

Quantity of ingredients:
Mustard 1/2 teaspoon / 1g. (yes)
Yogurt (natural, 3.5% fat) 1 cup / 250g. (yes)
Vinegar (Apple vinegar) 1 dash / 3g. (yes)
Celery root 1 1/2 piece / 900g. (yes)
Sour cream 15% fat 2 table spoons / 20g. (yes)
Peppers powder 1 pinch / 1g. (yes)
Onion white 1/2 piece / 25g. (yes)
Lemongrass 1 pinch / 1g. (yes)
Pepper (ground) 1 pinch / 0,5g. (yes)
Lemon juice 1 piece / 40g. (yes)
Salt 1 pinch / 1g. (little)
Sesame oil 1 table spoon / 20g. (yes)
Apple (sour) 1/2 piece / 100g. (yes)
Black caraway 1 pinch / 1g. (yes)
Turmeric (yellow root) 1 pinch / 1g. (yes)

Cooking instructions:
Cook the peeled celeriac in thick slices and then cut into bite-sized strips.

Dressing: Mix a little yoghurt, sour cream, turmeric, sesame oil, pepper, lemongrass powder, finely chopped onion, a little mustard, salt, crushed black cumin, some cold water, lemon juice or vinegar; add the sour chopped apple, some rose paprika, the lukewarm celery and mix well; let it rest for 2 - 3 hours or overnight.

Ideal as a substitute for raw food

9.13 Breakfast - Rice with fruits

Good to fight blood circulation disorders, thrombose, risk of embolism, high blood pressure, a headache, heart attack and stroke. Encourages blood build-up, promotes digestion, reduces Inflammation.
Cooking time approx. 10 min - 3 hours
Calories p. portion: 231
3 portions
Allergens: GHO

Quantity of ingredients:
Honey 1 table spoon / 10g. (yes)
Cinnamon ground 1 pinch / 1g. (yes)
Fig 1 table spoon / 15g. (yes)

Dates dried 1 table spoon / 15g. (yes)
Almond 1/2 teaspoon / 5g. (yes)
Hazelnuts 1/2 teaspoon / 5g. (little)
Butter Bio 1 table spoon / 15g. (little)
Basic recipe for a rice soup (Congee) 6 cups / 500g. (little)
Apple (sour) 1 piece / 200g. (yes)
Cow's milk (whole milk 3.5% fat) 1/2 to 1 cup / 80g. (yes)

Cooking instructions:
Cook rice congee according to basic recipe or use pre-cooked.
Make it with the milk more fluid and sweet with honey.
Fry the fruits and nuts in butter and mix with the finished rice soup, add
chopped dates, figs and the apple.

9.14 Broccoli and Parmesan spread on toast bread

Good to fight loss of appetite, blood clotting, thyroid function, increase
Vitamin B12, strengthen immune system, good to fight belching,
diabetes, acute or chronic constipation, dissolves stagnation.
Cooking time approx. 15 min
Calories p. portion: 148
2 portions
Allergens: AG

Quantity of ingredients:
Pepper (ground) 1 pinch / 0,3g. (yes)
Broccoli 5/8 oz / 200g. (yes)
Curd cheese 20% 3 oz / 80g. (little)
Toast bread (whole grain) 6 slices / 24g. (yes)
Salt 1 pinch / 1g. (little)
Chives 1 table spoon / 5g. (yes)
Basil (fresh) 1 table spoon / 5g. (yes)
Lemon peel 1/2 teaspoon / 1g. (yes)
Yogurt (natural, 1.5% fat) 1 table spoon / 10g. (yes)
Parmesan 2 table spoons / 15g. (little)

Cooking instructions:
Cook broccoli in a sieve insert over steam for 8 minutes until firm. Finely
chop broccoli.
Mix the curd, yoghurt, parmesan and lemon peel well. Mix cheese
cream with broccoli, basil and chives. Season the spread with salt and
pepper. Serve on the crunchy toasted toast.

9.15 Broccoli cream soup

Strengthen your immune system, build and maintain healthy bones, teeth, hair and nails. Reduces blood pressure, strengthens immune system, prevents cancer, reduces radiation damage.
Cooking time approx. 30 min
Calories p. portion: 98
6 portions
Allergens: LO

Quantity of ingredients:
Potato 2 pieces / 120g. (yes)
Broccoli 1,1 lbs / 500g. (yes)
Salt 1 pinch / 1g. (little)
Pepper (ground) 1 pinch / 0,5g. (yes)
Rosemary 1 teaspoon / 2g. (yes)
Basic recipe for a vegetable soup (nutritious) 2 cup / 500g. (yes)
Onion white 1 piece / 50g. (yes)
Water 1 cup / 50g. (yes)
Carrot 2 pieces / 150g. (yes)
Sage 1 teaspoon / 2g. (yes)
Olive oil 2 table spoons / 7g. (yes)
White wine 1/2 cup / 125g. (little)

Cooking instructions:
Add the olive oil to the pan, add the washed and cut broccoli, diced carrots and potatoes, sauté for a short time, add the chopped onion, fill with water, enough water to cover the vegetables at least 3 finger breadths. Add bouillon, salt, add a little bit of white wine, add the seasoned sage and rosemary.
Heat till it boils and then simmer on a small fire for about 25 minutes. Season with pepper, if necessary season with sea salt. Purée the soup.

9.16 Carrot and millet bake with apple compote

Promotes spleen and liver, reduces blood pressure, strengthens immune system, prevents cancer, reduces radiation damage, calms nerves and stomach, diuretic, good to fight chronic constipation of the intestine.
Cooking time approx. 1 hour
Calories p. portion: 350
7 portions
Allergens: CGH

Quantity of ingredients:
Cow's milk (whole milk 3.5% fat) 2 cups / 450g. (yes)
Butter Bio 1 teaspoon / 4g. (little)
Chicken egg 4 pieces / 240g. (little)
Acerola fruit nectar or powder 1 teaspoon / 2g. (yes)
Ginger fresh 2 teaspoons / 6g. (yes)
Carrot 7/8 lbs / 400g. (yes)
Lemon peel 1/2 piece / 2g. (yes)
Apple (sour) 4 pieces / 600g. (yes)
Yogurt (natural, 1.5% fat) 3/8 lbs - 6oz / 150g. (yes)
Sugar brown 2 table spoons / 20g. (yes)
Clove 2 pieces / 1g. (yes)
Sugar brown 1 table spoon / 10g. (yes)
Almond puree 1/8 lbs - 2oz / 50g. (yes)
Water 1 cup / 300g. (yes)
Millet 5/8 oz / 200g. (yes)

Cooking instructions:
Preheat the oven to 100°C/212°F (with circulating air 8o°C/176°F, gas level 2). Heat the milk with the millet till it boils, add lemon zest and sugar. Cover and simmer for 5 minutes, then simmer in a preheated oven for 20 minutes. Switch oven to medium heat.
Peel apples and cut into small pieces, boil with water, cloves and sugar for about 5 minutes.
Mix the millet in a bowl with the grated carrots, finely chopped ginger and acerola.
Mix the almond paste (or butter) with the hand mixer. Add egg yolk and stir everything to a smooth cream. Mix in sour cream. Add millet and carrots.
Beat the egg whites very stiff and lift them under the millet pulp. Brush out a baking dish with butter. Add the millet and bake in a preheated oven for 45 minutes on a low heat.
Serve with the apple compote.

9.17 Carrot and potato rucola sandwich

Reduces inflammation, improves digestion, supports urination, lowers cholesterol, strengthens immune system, prevents cancer, good to fight constipation (Fibre-rich), dissolves stagnation.
Cooking time approx. 20 min
Calories p. portion: 94
4 portions
Allergens: AG

Quantity of ingredients:
Lemon peel 1/4 teaspoon / 1g. (yes)
Whole grain bread 8 slices / 48g. (yes)
Salt 1 pinch / 1g. (little)
Rucola 1/2 bunch / 100g. (yes)
Onion (spring onion) 1 piece / 20g. (yes)
Sour cream 15% fat 2 table spoons / 45g. (yes)
Potato (mealy) 5/8 oz / 200g. (yes)
Carrot 1 piece / 50g. (yes)
Pepper (ground) 1 pinch / 0,2g. (yes)

Cooking instructions:
Cook the potatoes gently, peel and squeeze through the potato press.
Cook vegetable broth according to the basic recipe and remove a carrot
after a short cooking time and finely crush with a fork.
Stir the potatoes, carrots, grated lemon zest and sour cream into a
smooth cream. Mix carrot and potato cream with finely chopped rocket
salad. Season the spread with salt and pepper and spread the bread.
Sprinkle with the finely chopped young onions.

9.18 Carrot drink

Promotes spleen and liver, reduces blood pressure, strengthens
immune system, prevents cancer, reduces radiation damage, diuretic,
building up, eye-enhancing, detoxifying, nerve-strengthening.
Cooking time approx. 15 min
Calories p. portion: 143
1 portions
Allergens: H

Quantity of ingredients:
Water / 50g. (yes)
Millet flakes 1 table spoon / 10g. (yes)
Carrot 7/8 lbs / 200g. (yes)
Almond puree 1 teaspoon / 3g. (yes)
Honey 1/2 teaspoon / 2g. (yes)

Cooking instructions:
Sprinkle millet flakes with 50 ml of cold water and let it swell for 10
minutes. Juice the fresh carrots or use 200 ml. carrot juice.
Puree the millet flakes, carrot juice, almond paste and honey with the
blender.

9.19 Carrot Risotto

Strengthens immune system, prevents cancer, loss of appetite, flatulence, high blood pressure, depressions, diabetes, diarrhea, stimulates liver function, dissolves stagnation.
Cooking time approx. 45 min
Calories p. portion: 308
2 portions
Allergens: GL

Quantity of ingredients:
Parsley 1/2 bunch / 25g. (yes)
Salt 1 pinch / 1g. (little)
Pepper (ground) 1 pinch / 0,3g. (yes)
Parmesan 1 table spoon / 10g. (little)
Carrot 5/8 lbs - 8oz / 250g. (yes)
Rice variety any 1/4 lbs - 4oz / 100g. (yes)
Onion (spring onion) 2 table spoons / 7g. (yes)
Nutmeg 1 pinch / 0,3g. (yes)
Fennel seeds ground 1/4 teaspoon / 1g. (yes)
Olive oil 1/2 teaspoon / 5g. (yes)
Basil (fresh) 1/2 teaspoon / 2g. (yes)
Basic recipe for a vegetable soup (nutritious) 1 cup / 280g. (yes)

Cooking instructions:
Heat the oil in a pan, fry the onions in a glassy and very soft manner. Add parsley, sauté briefly. Add rice, carrots and nutmeg, sauté briefly while stirring. Add the vegetable stock, season with fennel and basil, heat till it boils and cook for about 20 minutes until the rice and carrots are well. Stir from time to time and add some vegetable stock if necessary. The risotto should be slightly soupy. Just before the end of the cooking time mix in the white wine and simmer the risotto for a short while. Remove risotto from the heat, mix in Parmesan.

9.20 Carrot soup

Promotes spleen and liver, reduces blood pressure, strengthens immune system, prevents cancer, reduces radiation damage, improves blood circulation, improves medication effect, increase Appetite, stimulates liver
Cooking time approx. 30 min
Calories p. portion: 210
2 portions
Allergens: O

Quantity of ingredients:
Pepper (ground) 1 pinch / 0,5g. (yes)
Carrot 1,1 lbs / 500g. (yes)
Nutmeg 1 pinch / 1g. (yes)
Salt 1 pinch / 1g. (little)
White wine 1/2 cup / 125g. (little)
Sunflower seeds Alternatively to pine nuts / g. (yes)
Peppers powder 1 pinch / 1g. (yes)
Thyme dried Alternative to rose paprika / g. (yes)
Pine nuts 1 table spoon / 15g. (yes)
Orange juice Alternatively for wine / g. (yes)
Parsley 2 table spoons / 10g. (yes)

Cooking instructions:
Place peeled large cut carrot pieces in hot water; cook and then puree; season with ground pepper, a little nutmeg, a pinch of salt; add a dash of white wine and simmer for a few minutes or season with orange juice; Add parsley as desired; stir in some rose paprika or fresh thyme; sprinkle with roasted pine nuts or sunflower seeds before serving.

9.21 Celery and potato cream soup

Reduces blood pressure, strengthens immune system, promotes weight loss. Good to fight immunodeficiency, loss of appetite, flatulence, depressions, diabetes, diarrhea, improves digestion.
Cooking time approx. 45 min
Calories p. portion: 113
4 portions
Allergens: GL

Quantity of ingredients:
Basic recipe for a vegetable soup (nutritious) 3 cups / 700g. (yes)
Ground 1 pinch / 0,5g. (yes)
Olive oil 1 table spoon / 10g. (yes)
Lemon peel 1/4 piece / 1g. (yes)
Crème fraiche cheese 2 table spoons / 20g. (little)
Salt 1 pinch / 1g. (little)
Onion white 1/2 piece / 25g. (yes)
Potato 5/8 oz / 200g. (yes)
Nutmeg 1 pinch / 0,5g. (yes)
Parsley 1 table spoon / 8g. (yes)

Cooking instructions:
Heat the olive oil in a saucepan lightly. Fry the onions very gently in a mild heat. Pour with vegetable stock according to the basic recipe. Cover and cook for 15 minutes.
Add curd-cut potato, celery, nutmeg, cumin and lemon zest. Spice with salt and cook for 12 minutes. Potatoes and celery should be soft. Remove the lemon peel.
Puree the soup with crème fraiche using a blender. Season the soup with salt.
Arrange the soup in portions with the chopped parsley.

9.22 Celery soup

Forcing spleen, calms nerves, stimulates appetite and digestion, dissolves stagnation.
Cooking time approx. 45 min
Calories p. portion: 101
4 portions
Allergens: ACGL

Quantity of ingredients:
Pepper (ground) 1 pinch / 0,5g. (yes)
Water 2 cup / 500g. (yes)
Nutmeg 1 pinch / 1g. (yes)
Salt 1 pinch / 1g. (little)
Butter Bio 1 table spoon / 15g. (little)
Celery root 1 piece / 500g. (yes)
Chicken egg 1 piece / 55g. (little)
Celery sticks 2 table spoons / 20g. (yes)
Spelled wholemeal flour 2-3 teaspoons / 25g. (yes)
Cream sour 10% 2 table spoons / 25g. (yes)

Cooking instructions:
In a hot saucepan, melt 1 tbsp butter; add a pinch of nutmeg, a pinch of salt, 1/2 cup wholegrain spelled flour (finely ground as fresh as possible) and stir to a sweat while stirring; add 1/2 liter of hot water gradually; add 1 large finely chopped celery tuber; cook for about 35 minutes and then puree; mix 1 egg yolk with 1 cup of cream; in the hot - no longer boiling! - soup vigorously; add some celery leaves finely chopped; with pepper, salt to taste.

9.23 Champignon rice

Strengthens kidney, diuretic, warming the body from the inside, expands blood vessels, strengthens the muscles, promotes digestion and is good to fight high blood pressure, dissolves stagnation, promotes weight loss. Good to fight immunodeficiency, loss of appetite.
Cooking time approx. 30 min
Calories p. portion: 410
2 portions
Allergens: L

Quantity of ingredients:
Onion white 1 piece / 50g. (yes)
Pepper (ground) 1 pinch / 0,2g. (yes)
Parsley 1/2 oz / 20g. (yes)
Champignon 1/8 lbs - 2oz / 60g. (yes)
Basic recipe for a vegetable soup (nutritious) 7/8 lbs / 350g. (yes)
Clove 2 pieces / 1g. (yes)
Rice (whole grain) 5/8 oz / 200g. (yes)
Bay leaf 2 pieces / 1g. (yes)

Cooking instructions:
Plug in the cloves in the onion. Heat the vegetable stock with the onion and the bay leaves till it boils. Add the rice to the boiling liquid, reduce the temperature to the lowest level and stir with the lid closed for 20-25 minutes.
In the meantime, wash the mushrooms, clean them, slice them, sauté briefly with a little water or sauté. Wash the parsley and chop finely. Remove the onion from the rice, add the mushrooms and the parsley, season with pepper.

9.24 Chicory salad with tangerine

Dissolves mucus, is rich in A-B-C Vitamins, promotes digestion, forcing spleen, promotes weight loss. Good to fight loss of appetite, flatulence, immunodeficiency.
Cooking time approx. 10 min
Calories p. portion: 257
3 portions
Allergens: AGNO

Quantity of ingredients:
Orange jam 1 teaspoon / 4g. (yes)
Tangerine 4 pieces / 300g. (yes)

Chicory 2-3 pieces / 300g. (yes)
Sesame oil 2 table spoons / 18g. (yes)
Salt 1 pinch / 1g. (little)
Cream, sweet 30% 1 table spoon / 10g. (little)
Pepper (ground) 1 pinch / 0,5g. (yes)
Vinegar Aceto Balsamico 2 teaspoons / 6g. (yes)
Orange 1/2 piece / 70g. (yes)
Lemon 1/2 piece / 25g. (yes)
Peppers powder 1 pinch / 1g. (yes)
White bread (wheat bread) 6 slices / 120g. (yes)

Cooking instructions:
Peel tangerines and cut into bite-sized pieces; Cut chicory roughly and mix well.
Dressing: sesame oil, pepper, salt, raspberry vinegar or balsamic vinegar, a little lemon or orange juice, rose paprika, orange marmalade or, alternatively, another jam, stir well. Give a little sweet cream over the salad and let it pass briefly.

9.25 Cold cherry soup with curd cheese dumpling

Improves blood circulation, reduces inflammation, good to fight weakness, belching, diabetes, acute or chronic obstruction of the bowel. Laxative, stimulates digestion, cleans the intestinal flora.
Cooking time approx. 2 hours and more
Calories p. portion: 320
2 portions
Allergens: GO

Quantity of ingredients:
Cherry compote 7/8 lbs / 450g. (yes)
Lemon peel 1 pinch / 1g. (yes)
Cinnamon ground 1 pinch / 0,5g. (yes)
Vanilla sugar natural 1 package / 1g. (yes)
Sour cream 15% fat 1/8 lbs - 2oz / 50g. (yes)
Agar agar (kelp) 1/2 teaspoon / 1,5g. (yes)
Sugar brown 1 table spoon / 10g. (yes)
Curd cheese 20% 1/4 lbs - 4oz / 100g. (little)

Cooking instructions:
Strain the cherry compote.
Finely puree half of the cherries with the cherry juice using a blender and pass through a sieve.

Stir agar agar powder with cold water until smooth.
Bring the cherry puree to boil while stirring.
Mix in the agar-agar and cook the cherry puree for 1 minute while stirring.
Spread hot cherry puree on two soup plates.
Sprinkle the remaining cherries into the soup.
Cool down cherry soup for 2 hours until lightly gelled.
Use the hand mixer to stir the cord cheese, sour cream, sugar, vanilla sugar, cinnamon and lemon zest into a smooth, firm cream.
From the cream with the tablespoon, prick small dumplings and put them into the cherry soup.

9.26 Compote of pears

Pear benefits digestion, supports urination. Cocoa forces liver, strengthens the muscles, strengthens the defense. Good to fight fungi infections.
Cooking time approx. 10 min
Calories p. portion: 122
4 portions
Allergens:

Quantity of ingredients:
Pear 4 pieces / 800g. (yes)
Anise (Common Fennel) 1/2 teaspoon / 1g. (yes)
Vanilla pod 1 pinch / 1g. (yes)
Water 1 cup / 280g. (yes)
Cocoa 1 pinch / 1g. (little)

Cooking instructions:
Boil pears (organic - with peel), aniseed, vanilla, chili soft. Sprinkle with cocoa.

9.27 Corn coffee with cardamom

Diuretic, forcing spleen, supports urination, relaxes, reduces fat.
Cooking time approx. 5 min
Calories p. portion: 3
1 portions
Allergens:

Quantity of ingredients:
Water 1 cup / 120g. (yes)
Cereal coffee 1 table spoon / 15g. (yes)
Cardamom 2 cores / 1g. (yes)

Cooking instructions:
Boil water, coffee, sugar and cardamom. Let it set for one min before drinking.

9.28 Zucchini with basil pesto

Good to fight bloating and nausea. Relaxing and reassuring, promotes digestion, forcing spleen and digestive system, detoxifying, strengthens the muscles and bones, diuretic, supports urination, dissolves stagnation.
Cooking time approx. 25 min
Calories p. portion: 468
3 portions
Allergens: ACGHL

Quantity of ingredients:
Salt 1 pinch / 1g. (little)
Ground 1 pinch / 1g. (yes)
Oregano dried 2 teaspoons / 15g. (yes)
Zucchini 5/8 lbs - 8oz / 250g. (yes)
Onion (spring onion) 2 pieces / 40g. (yes)
Olive oil 1 table spoon / 15g. (yes)
Noodles (wheat, spaghetti) with egg 5/8 oz / 200g. (yes)
Pepper (ground) 1 pinch / 1g. (yes)
Salt 1 pinch / 1g. (little)
Lemon 1 teaspoon / 3g. (yes)
Lemon peel 1 teaspoon / 3g. (yes)
Basic recipe for a vegetable soup (nutritious) 2 table spoons / 45g. (yes)
Olive oil 1 table spoon / 20g. (yes)
Almond 1 table spoon / 15g. (yes)
Parmesan 1 oz / 30g. (little)
Basil (fresh) 1 Bunch / 125g. (yes)

Cooking instructions:
Mix Basil, olive oil, grated almonds, parmesan, vegetable broth and grated lemon peel to a smooth cream puree.
Season the pesto with salt, oregano, cumin and pepper.

Boil the spaghetti with a little salt in plenty of water.
Heat the olive oil in a pan and fry the spring onions while stirring. Add zucchini and fry briefly with stirring. The zucchini should be soft with a bite. Season the zucchini with salt.
In a bowl, mix well-drained spaghetti with zucchini and pesto. Season the spaghetti with salt and pepper.
Recommended for dysphagia, loss of appetite, potassium and magnesium requirements.

9.29 Couscous Salad

prevents cancer, forcing spleen, promotes digestion, stimulates liver function, reduces blood pressure, strengthens immune system, reduces radiation damage, diuretic.
Cooking time approx. 25 min
Calories p. portion: 338
3 portions
Allergens: A

Quantity of ingredients:
Lemon juice 2 table spoons / 30g. (yes)
Carrot 1/4 lbs - 4oz / 100g. (yes)
Cucumber 1/4 lbs - 4oz / 100g. (yes)
Olive oil 1 table spoon / 15g. (yes)
Tomato 2 pieces / 80g. (yes)
Couscous 5/8 oz / 200g. (yes)
Parsley 1 Bunch / 100g. (yes)
Lemon peel 1 teaspoon / 2g. (yes)
Chives 1 Bunch / 100g. (yes)
Peppermint 3 twigs / 30g. (yes)
Water 1 cup / 100g. (yes)

Cooking instructions:
Boil in a small saucepan 250 ml. water with salt and 1 tablespoon olive oil. Add the couscous, take the stove in the front and let it swell covered for 5 minutes. Put the couscous back on the stove and let it simmer for about 2 minutes with gentle stirring. If necessary, add 1 - 3 tbsp of hot water.
Mix the couscous with lemon juice, chopped lemon peel and 1 tbsp oil, season with salt and pepper and leave to set.
Add couscous with tomatoes, cucumber, parsley (all diced), carrots (grated), chives and mint (finely chopped).
Season the couscous salad with lemon juice, salt and pepper.

9.30 Cranberry juice

Antibacterial, good to fight loss of appetite, arteriosclerosis, bladder infections, diarrhea, colds. Antipyretic, against free radicals, gout, diuretic, stomach ulcers, oral mucosa inflammation, rheumatism.
Cooking time approx. 5 min
Calories p. portion: 43
1 portions
Allergens:

Quantity of ingredients:
Cranberries 2 table spoons / 25g. (recommended)
Water 1 cup / 125g. (yes)
Honey 1 table spoon / 10g. (yes)

Cooking instructions:
Mix the cranberries with a little water with the blender to a pulp. Add the remaining water and sweeten with the honey.

9.31 Cucumber salad

Diuretic, detoxifying, suppresses conversion of sugar into fat, lowers cholesterol, prevents cancer. Cucumber cools and moistens. Dill works against flatulence, anticonvulsant in gastrointestinal discomfort.
Cooking time approx. 5 min
Calories p. portion: 27
2 portions
Allergens: O

Quantity of ingredients:
Cucumber 1 piece / 400g. (yes)
Dill 1 pinch / 1g. (yes)
Vinegar (Apple vinegar) 1 table spoon / 10g. (yes)
Salt 1 pinch / 1g. (little)

Cooking instructions:
Cut the cucumber (do not peel the BIO) thinly and season.

9.32 Cucumber soup

Diuretic, detoxifying, suppresses conversion of sugar into fat, lowers cholesterol, prevents cancer, promotes digestion, diaphoretic, dries out, good to fight yeast infections.
Cooking time approx. 20 min
Calories p. portion: 96
4 portions
Allergens: M

Quantity of ingredients:
Water 2 cup / 500g. (yes)
Cucumber 2 pieces / 400g. (yes)
Sage 3 leaves / 3g. (yes)
Salt 1 pinch / 1g. (little)
Olive oil 2 table spoons / 35g. (yes)
Cardamom 1 pinch / 1g. (yes)
Coriander 1 pinch / 1g. (yes)
Mustard 1/2 teaspoon / 0,5g. (yes)

Cooking instructions:
Heat oil and roast short the small cucumbers. Add Mustard seeds, coriander, cardamom and salt. Add water.
Simmer for 10-15 min. Puree and decorate with fresh chopped sage.

9.33 Curry rice with raisins and nuts

Stops diarrhea, promotes digestion, appetizing, harmonizes the stomach, improves blood circulation, improves medication effect, stimulates appetite, detoxifies the skin, stimulates nerves, frees breathing, increases body temperature, promotes perspiration.
Cooking time approx. 30 min
Calories p. portion: 275
4 portions
Allergens: HO

Quantity of ingredients:
Sunflower oil 1 table spoon / 15g. (yes)
Lemon Alternatively for white wine / g. (yes)
Walnuts 2 table spoons / 25g. (little)
Peppers powder 1 pinch / 1g. (yes)
Apple (sweet) 2 pieces / 300g. (yes)
Onion white 1 piece / 50g. (yes)
White wine 1/2 cup / 125g. (little)

Raisins 2 table spoons / 25g. (yes)
Water 6 cups / 500g. (yes)
Rice wild (nature rice) 1 cup / 120g. (yes)
Curry 1/2 teaspoon / 2g. (yes)
Salt 1 pinch / 1g. (little)

Cooking instructions:
Heat oil in a pot; fry chopped onions until glassy; add the curry and let it
foam for a short time; then fry the raw rice for a few minutes over a
gentle heat, stirring constantly; Salt, a dash of white wine or lemon
juice, rose paprika, sweet apples chopped, raisins, chopped, roasted
nuts added; pour hot water on it until well covered; simmer until the rice
is cooked.

Goes well with: carrot and fennel vegetables, legumes with boiled
vegetables, sliced poultry with ginger and mushrooms.

9.34 Delicately spiced zucchini with tomatoes

Diuretic, promotes digestion, helps to digest fat, reduces blood
pressure, dissolves stagnation, antioxidativ,
supports urination, diuretic, warming the body from the inside, expands
blood vessels.
Cooking time approx. 10 min
Calories p. portion: 203
4 portions
Allergens:

Quantity of ingredients:
Zucchini 4 pieces / 800g. (yes)
Rice (whole grain) 1 cup / 120g. (yes)
Water 6 cups / 400g. (yes)
Salt 1 pinch / 1g. (little)
Onion white 2 pieces / 120g. (yes)
Basil (fresh) 6-8 leaves / 3g. (yes)
Salt 1 pinch / 1g. (little)
Olive oil 1 table spoon / 20g. (yes)
Tomato 2 pieces / 120g. (yes)
Oregano dried 1 pinch / 1g. (yes)

Cooking instructions:
In a hot pan, fry olive oil, finely chopped onions and finely chopped
zucchini until half cooked. Add plenty of dried oregano. Salt and chop

the tomatoes for a few minutes until the zucchini are tender but crisp. Add fresh basil as desired.

Variation: Put some sheep's cheese over the tomatoes and finish cooking with the lid closed.

Place the rice in salted water, heat till it boils and let it simmer over low heat for about 15 minutes.

9.35 Fennel and potato gratin

Reduces inflammation, improves blood circulation, improves digestion, supports urination, lowers cholesterol, good to fight loss of appetite, flatulence, inflammatory bowel disease, heartburn. Forcing spleen, improves blood circulation.
Cooking time approx. 1 1/2 hours
Calories p. portion: 147
2 portions
Allergens: CGL

Quantity of ingredients:
Salt 1 pinch / 1g. (little)
Chives 1 teaspoon / 3g. (yes)
Parsley 1 teaspoon / 2g. (yes)
Pepper Cayenne 1 pinch / 0,5g. (yes)
Potato 1/4 lbs - 4oz / 125g. (yes)
Butter Bio 1 teaspoon / 3g. (little)
Parmesan 1 teaspoon / 3g. (little)
Basic recipe for a vegetable soup (nutritious) 1/2 cup / 100g. (yes)
Nutmeg 1 pinch / 0,5g. (yes)
Chicken yolk 1 piece / 10g. (little)
Fennel 5/8 oz / 200g. (yes)
Rice flour 2 teaspoons / 6g. (yes)
Cream sour 10% 1 teaspoon / 3g. (yes)
Sugar cane sugar 1 pinch / 1g. (yes)
Butter Bio 1 teaspoon / 3g. (little)

Cooking instructions:
Cook peeled potatoes and then let cool. Wash the fennel, cut off the stems and remove any outer leaves.
Hold back fennel greens and add it to the sauce with the other herbs later.

Steam the fennel tubers for about 15 - 20 minutes.
Then cut the potatoes and fennel into slices and place in layers in a greased baking dish.
Bring the liquid of fennel broth to the boil and bind it with flour.
Season with sea salt, cayenne pepper, sugar, nutmeg and sour cream.
Allow to cool and alloy with egg yolk.
Spread the sauce over the casserole, sprinkle with parmesan and finely chopped parsley and chives. Bake at 200°C / 392°F in the oven for half an hour.

9.36 Fennel-Rice Soup

Forcing spleen, relieves constipation, stimulates nerves, detoxifying, reduces inflammation, improves blood circulation.
Cooking time approx. 15-20 min
Calories p. portion: 156
2 portions
Allergens: EG

Quantity of ingredients:
Basic recipe for a rice soup (Congee) 1 cup / 300g. (little)
Soy sauce 1 dash / 3g. (little)
Fennel 1/2 piece / 150g. (yes)
Butter Bio 1 table spoon / 15g. (little)

Cooking instructions:
Cook the fennel softly in the rice soup according to the basic recipe.
Before serving, add a piece of butter and some soy sauce.

9.37 Fried asparagus with rocket

Diuretic, improves blood circulation, prevents cancer, stimulates digestion, forcing spleen, promotes weight loss. Good to fight immunodeficiency, loss of appetite, arteriosclerosis, flatulence, bladder weakness, anemia, high blood pressure, depressions, diabetes.
Cooking time approx. 15 min
Calories p. portion: 149
3 portions
Allergens: G

Quantity of ingredients:
Rucola 2 handful / 30g. (yes)
Potato 3/4 lbs / 300g. (yes)
Salt 1 pinch / 1g. (little)
Pepper (ground) 1 pinch / 0,5g. (yes)
Lemon 1/4 piece / 12g. (yes)
Asparagus (green or white) 1,1 lbs / 500g. (yes)
Butter Bio 1 table spoon / 20g. (little)

Cooking instructions:
Melt a piece of butter in a hot pan; cut the peeled asparagus into pieces of 3 to 4 cm, fry for about 10 minutes until tender, but crisp. Sprinkle with freshly ground pepper, salt, add a few drops of lemon juice or finely grated lemon zest, finely shredded rucola leaves.
Cook the potatoes in plenty of salted water, then peel.

9.38 Fruit juice

Stops diarrhea, promotes digestion, appetizing, harmonizes the stomach, relieves pain, detoxifying, reduces blood pressure, strengthens immune system, prevents cancer, reduces radiation damage.
Cooking time approx. 10 min
Calories p. portion: 176
2 portions
Allergens:

Quantity of ingredients:
Apple (sweet) 4 pieces / 300g. (yes)
Honey 1 table spoon / 10g. (yes)
Orange 2 pieces / 150g. (yes)
Carrot 2 pieces / 150g. (yes)

Cooking instructions:
Peel oranges and carrots. Cut all ingredients into cubes so that they fit into the juicer and juice. Sweet with honey.

9.39 Hearty polenta mash

Strengths spleen and stomach, promotes watering, promotes digestion, detoxifying, promotes perspiration, reduces blood lipids, stimulates, dissolves stagnation, stimulates appetite, dissolves stagnation.
Cooking time approx. 10 min
Calories p. portion: 262
2 portions
Allergens:

Quantity of ingredients:
Corn Grease (Polenta) 1 cup / 120g. (yes)
Onion (spring onion) 2 pieces / 40g. (yes)
Ginger fresh 1/2 teaspoon / 2g. (yes)
Salt 1 pinch / 1g. (little)
Water 1 1/2 cups / 240g. (yes)
Nutmeg 1 pinch / 1g. (yes)
Olive oil 1 table spoon / 10g. (yes)
Turmeric (yellow root) 1 pinch / 1g. (yes)

Cooking instructions:
Stir in the polenta in boiling water and let it swell for 7 min. Add green onion, grated ginger, turmeric, nutmeg, salt and olive oil and wait for 3 more minutes.

9.40 Kohlrabi in curry sauce with potatoes

Reduces inflammation, lowers cholesterol, diuretic, conducts bowel winds, strengthens immune system, prevents cancer, promotes weight loss. Good to fight loss of appetite, flatulence, high blood pressure, depressions, diabetes, diarrhea.
Cooking time approx. 1 hour
Calories p. portion: 188
4 portions
Allergens: GL

Quantity of ingredients:
Pepper (ground) 1 pinch / 0,2g. (yes)
Chervil dried 1 Bunch / 80g. (yes)
Lemon peel 1/2 teaspoon / 2g. (yes)
Sour cream 15% fat 2 table spoons / 30g. (yes)
Potato 1/4 lbs - 4oz / 100g. (yes)

Salt 1 pinch / 1g. (little)
Kohlrabi 3/4 lbs / 300g. (yes)
Lovage 1/2 teaspoon / 2g. (yes)
Ginger fresh 1/2 teaspoon / 2g. (yes)
Nutmeg 1 pinch / 0,2g. (yes)
Potato 6 pieces / 450g. (yes)
Basic recipe for a vegetable soup (nutritious) 1 cup / 300g. (yes)

Cooking instructions:
Boil the potatoes in salted water.
Bring half of the vegetable stock to boil. Add the diced potatoes, nutmeg, lemon zest, ginger and lovage. Cover the potatoes and cook for about 10 minutes until soft and puree them with a blender until they are smooth.
Bring remaining vegetable stock to boil. Cut kohlrabi into cubes and add, cover and cook for about 8 minutes. Stir in the potato sauce and heat everything briefly.
Puree with the mixing stick chervil and sour cream. Mix the chervil cream with the kohlrabi vegetables.
Serve with the cooked, peeled potatoes.

9.41 Lettuce with fresh cheese

The bitter substances have diuretic effect and promote the blood circulation in the digestive area. Mustard improves thyroid function, relieves rheumatism symptoms.
Cooking time approx. 5 min
Calories p. portion: 802
1 portions
Allergens: AFM

Quantity of ingredients:
Mustard 1 knife tip / 1g. (yes)
Lemon juice 1 dash / 3g. (yes)
Fresh cheese from soya 3/8 lbs - 6oz / 150g. (yes)
Whole grain bread 2 slices / 40g. (yes)
Leaf salads (bitter) 2 portions / 60g. (yes)
Pepper (ground) 1 pinch / 0,5g. (yes)
Herbs various 2 teaspoons / 4g. (yes)
Salt 1 pinch / 1g. (little)
Black caraway 1 pinch / 1g. (yes)

Cooking instructions:
Wash lettuce and finely pluck.
Mix 150 ml cream cheese, splashes of mustard, splashes of lemon juice, 1 clove of garlic, chopped fresh herbs, pinch of pepper and crushed black cumin and pour over. Serve with wholemeal bread.

9.42 Millet with pears

Refreshing and nourishing, promotes digestion, supports urination, good to fight cough, promotes perspiration, reduces blood lipids, stimulates, dissolves stagnation, forces liver, strengthens the muscles, lowers cholesterol, antiparasitic.
Cooking time approx. 35 min
Calories p. portion: 213
5 portions
Allergens: G

Quantity of ingredients:
Ginger fresh 1/2 teaspoon / 2g. (yes)
Cocoa 1 pinch / 1g. (little)
Water 1 1/2 cups / 200g. (yes)
Sunflower seeds 2 table spoons / 4g. (yes)
Barley malt 1/2 teaspoon / 2g. (yes)
Grape juice red 1 1/2 cups / 240g. (yes)
Millet 1 cup / 120g. (yes)
Pear 4 pieces / 600g. (yes)
Acerola fruit nectar or powder 1 teaspoon / 2g. (yes)
Salt 1 pinch / 1g. (little)
Cream, sweet 30% 2 teaspoons / 20g. (little)

Cooking instructions:
Simmer the millet for 5 min and let it swell for another 30 min.

Then: In a hot pot, heat some grape juice; add chopped pears, very little grated ginger, a pinch of salt, acerola, a pinch of cocoa and sauté briefly; add the boiled millet, sunflower seeds, some barley malt to taste, 1 tsp cream per serving or a little butter.

9.43 Noodles with vegetable and tomato sauce

Protects the digestive system. Detoxifying, Good to fight loss of appetite, flatulence, inflammatory bowel disease, obesity, gout, stomach ulcers, stomach cramps, rheumatism, heartburn, twelffinger intestinal ulcers, promotes digestion, helps to digest fat.
Cooking time approx. 45 min
Calories p. portion: 562
2 portions
Allergens: ACG

Quantity of ingredients:
Oregano dried 1 pinch / 1g. (yes)
Olive oil 1 table spoon / 10g. (yes)
Onion (shallot) 1 piece / 20g. (yes)
Olive oil 1 table spoon / 15g. (yes)
Zucchini 1 piece / 80g. (yes)
Carrot 1 piece / 80g. (yes)
Tomato 1/4 lbs - 4oz / 125g. (yes)
Noodles (wheat) with egg 5/8 oz / 200g. (yes)
Pepper (ground) 1 pinch / 0,2g. (yes)
Creme fraiche cheese 2 table spoons / 30g. (little)
Salt 1 pinch / 1g. (little)

Cooking instructions:
Boil the tomatoes with a little water, drain and collect the juice, cut the tomatoes into pieces.
Roughly grate zucchini and carrot. Heat olive oil in a pot. Steam shallots very soft. Add tomatoes, season with oregano, salt and pepper. Simmer tomatoes to a thick sauce.
Bring plenty of salted water to boil, cook the wholegrain noodles until firm. In the cooking time of the pasta, heat in a pan olive oil. Fry the carrots while stirring, lightly salt. Add zucchini, sauté briefly while stirring. The vegetables should be soft with a bite.
Drain pasta, mix with crème fraiche, season with salt and pepper. Garnish with the tomato sauce.

9.44 Oat Congee

Strengthens immune system.
Cooking time approx. 2-4 hours
Calories p. portion: 162
3 portions
Allergens: A

Quantity of ingredients:
Water 6 cups / 700g. (yes)
Oat 1 cup / 125g. (yes)

Cooking instructions:
Cook oats and water in a ratio of about 1: 6. The amount of water determines the thickness of the mash (pure matter of taste). The oats swell, so do not take much. Put the oats in a saucepan with good insulation and a heavy lid. It is important to simmer the oats after a short boil on the slightest flame, otherwise it burns. Cook the oat for 2-4 hours. The longer it cooks, the more he strengthens.

9.45 Oat flakes with aromatic spices

Stops diarrhea, promotes digestion, appetizing, harmonizes the stomach, relieves diarrhea, strengthens immune system, detoxifying and stimulating the immune system.
Cooking time approx. 25 min
Calories p. portion: 280
3 portions
Allergens: AH

Quantity of ingredients:
Oat flakes (whole grain) 1 cup / 125g. (yes)
Water 1 1/2 cups / 240g. (yes)
Cardamom 3-4 capsules / 2g. (yes)
Lemon Balm (fresh) 3-4 leaves / 3g. (yes)
Walnuts 1 table spoon / 15g. (little)
Apple (sweet) 1 piece / 220g. (yes)
Hazelnuts 1 table spoon / 15g. (little)
Wakame 1 inch / 2g. (yes)
Acerola fruit nectar or powder 1 teaspoon / 2g. (yes)

Cooking instructions:
Roast oatmeal and nuts. Add hot water. Add cardamom, wakame and cook for 20 min. Add grated apple, acerola and lemon herb.

9.46 Oatmeal soup with spring onion and carrots

Reduces blood pressure, strengthens immune system, prevents cancer, reduces radiation damage, stimulates digestion, reduces pain, stimulates appetite, dissolves stagnation.
Cooking time approx. 30 min
Calories p. portion: 135
3 portions
Allergens: AG

Quantity of ingredients:
Carrot 2 pieces / 200g. (yes)
Oat 6 table spoons / 48g. (yes)
Butter Bio 1 table spoon / 15g. (little)
Nutmeg 1 pinch / 1g. (yes)
Lovage 1 stem / 15g. (yes)
Onion (spring onion) 2 pieces / 40g. (yes)
Water 2 cup / 480g. (yes)

Cooking instructions:
Roast the oats in butter, add salt and spices, pour in water and heat till it boils. After 10 min. add the grated carrots and lovage, cook for 10 minutes. Finely add chopped onion.

9.47 Oriental rice pan

Forcing spleen, dissolves stagnation, promotes weight loss. Good to fight immunodeficiency, loss of appetite, flatulence, high blood pressure, helps to digest fat, strengthens kidney and bladder.
Numerous vitamins, minerals and secondary plant active ingredients.
Cooking time approx. 30 min
Calories p. portion: 303
6 portions
Allergens: EL

Quantity of ingredients:
Peas 3 oz / 80g. (yes)
Rice (whole grain) 3/8 lbs - 6oz / 180g. (yes)
Tomato 5/8 oz / 200g. (yes)
Pineapple 1/8 lbs - 2oz / 60g. (yes)
Peppers 1/4 lbs - 4oz / 120g. (yes)
Pepper (ground) 1 pinch / 1g. (yes)

Peaches 1/8 lbs - 2oz / 60g. (yes)
Bamboo shoots 3 oz / 80g. (yes)
Shiitake, dried 1/2 oz / 80g. (yes)
Basic recipe for a vegetable soup (nutritious) 2 1/4 cups / 500g. (yes)
Lemon Balm (fresh) 1 teaspoon / 2g. (yes)
Curry 1/2 teaspoon / 2g. (yes)
Onion (spring onion) 4 pieces / 80g. (yes)
Rapeseed oil 2 table spoons / 20g. (yes)
Lovage 1 teaspoon / 2g. (yes)
Basil (fresh) 1 teaspoon / 2g. (yes)
Parsley 1 teaspoon / 2g. (yes)
Corn 3 oz / 80g. (yes)

Cooking instructions:
Soak the mushrooms in water 20 min.
Boil the rice in the vegetable stock 15 min. and season with some curry.
Peel the onion, cut into fine cubes.
Heat the oil in a pan and sauté the onion cubes.
Wash the peppers in half, remove the core, cut into cubes and add.
Add corn, mushrooms and bamboo shoots, simmer 5 min. until firm.
Also add the bean sprouts, peas, peach cubes and pineapple cubes.
Then add the peeled, chopped tomatoes.
Add the cooked rice and season with the herbs and pepper.

9.48 Paprika-tomato rice

Good to fight little cholesterol, diabetes. Low in protein, low fat content, little protein. Forcing spleen, dissolves stagnation, promotes weight loss. Good to fight immunodeficiency, loss of appetite, flatulence, high blood pressure, depressions.
Cooking time approx. 25 min
Calories p. portion: 291
3 portions
Allergens: L

Quantity of ingredients:
Parsley 1/2 oz / 20g. (yes)
Onion white 1 piece / 50g. (yes)
Tomato 1/4 lbs - 4oz / 120g. (yes)
Pepper (ground) 1 pinch / 0,2g. (yes)
Champignon 1/8 lbs - 2oz / 60g. (yes)

Rice (whole grain) 5/8 oz / 200g. (yes)
Basic recipe for a vegetable soup (nutritious) 7/8 lbs / 400g. (yes)
Clove 2 pieces / 1g. (yes)
Bay leaf 2 pieces / 1g. (yes)
Peppers 4 pieces / 120g. (yes)
Peppers (rose peppers) 1 pinch / 0,2g. (yes)

Cooking instructions:
Finely chop the onion. Cut the peppers into fine strips.
Heat margarine in a saucepan, sauté onions and peppers, and rice.
Add the vegetable stock, add cloves and bay leaves and leave to
simmer in a closed pot for approx. 20 minutes. Cut the tomato meat into
1 cm cubes and add to the rice 5 minutes before the end of cooking.

9.49 Pear juice

Promotes digestion, supports urination.
Cooking time approx. 5 min
Calories p. portion: 180
2 portions
Allergens:

Quantity of ingredients:
Pear 3 pieces / 600g. (yes)

Cooking instructions:
Peel pears thinly (vitamins under the skin) and core. Juice in the juicer.

9.50 Plum Cake

Cancer preventive effect, dehydrates the body, stimulates digestion and
binds fats in the intestine, good to fight loss of appetite, flatulence,
inflammatory bowel disease, obesity, gout, stomach ulcers, stomach
cramps, rheumatism, heartburn. Relieves pain, detoxifying, bactericide.
Cooking time approx. 1 hour
Calories p. portion: 502
6 portions
Allergens: AG

Quantity of ingredients:
Salt 1 pinch / 1g. (little)
Plums 2,2 lbs / 1000g. (yes)
Curd cheese 20% 5/8 oz / 200g. (little)
Wheat flour 7/8 lbs / 400g. (yes)

Cow's milk (whole milk 3.5% fat) 6 table spoons / 70g. (yes)
Rapeseed oil 6 table spoons / 70g. (yes)
Baking powder 1 package / 3g. (yes)
Cinnamon ground 1 teaspoon / 3g. (yes)
Honey 8 table spoons / 100g. (yes)

Cooking instructions:
Mix the flour, curd cheese, milk, oil, honey, salt and baking powder into a smooth dough. Keep the dough cool for 15 minutes to cool.
Lay out baking paper on a baking sheet and press the dough out to a bottom.
Now spread the plums evenly.
Sprinkle the cake with the cinnamon and bake for about 40 minutes at 190 ° C/374 °F.

9.51 Polenta with peach

Relieves fatigue, forcing spleen, diuretic, strengthens the defense, good to fight fungi infections, lets urine and bile juice flow, prevents the aging process, strengthens brain cells.
Cooking time approx. 20 min
Calories p. portion: 197
3 portions
Allergens:

Quantity of ingredients:
Peaches 2-3 pieces / 400g. (yes)
Water 1 1/2 cups / 240g. (yes)
Corn Grease (Polenta) 1 cup / 120g. (yes)
Cinnamon ground 1 pinch / 1g. (yes)
Vanilla pod 1 pinch / 1g. (yes)

Cooking instructions:
Pour the polenta into a pan of hot water with constant stirring until the polenta has the desired consistency. Pull the polenta from the fire and let it soak for 10 minutes.

Wash fresh peaches and cut into quarters. Pour into the finished polenta the peaches, add the vanilla and add Chili to taste, stir and let it go for 3 minutes.

Winter varieties: Pickled fruit, pear, apples

9.52 Porridge with raisins and sake

Strengthens immune system, improves blood circulation, improves medication effect, stimulates appetite, detoxifies the skin, stimulates nerves, frees breathing, increases body temperature, promotes perspiration.
Cooking time approx. 10 min
Calories p. portion: 427
1 portions
Allergens: AGO

Quantity of ingredients:
Oat flakes (whole grain) 8 table spoons / 60g. (yes)
Cow's milk (whole milk 3.5% fat) 1/2 cup / 125g. (yes)
Cream, sweet 30% 2 table spoons / 20g. (little)
Raisins 1 table spoon / 15g. (yes)
Water 1/2 cup / 125g. (yes)
Salt 1 pinch / 1g. (little)
Sake 1 table spoon / 10g. (yes)

Cooking instructions:
Heat water and milk and a pinch of salt till it boils. Sprinkle in 4 tablespoons of coarse rolled oats and cook to a pulp, add 4 tablespoons of fine oatmeal, allow to simmer. Arrange in a preheated bowl and top with cream.
Add raisins and sake.

9.53 Potato gnocchi with vegetables and basil sauce

Strengthens immune system, promotes weight loss. Good to fight immunodeficiency, loss of appetite, flatulence, high blood pressure. Relaxing and reassuring.
Cooking time approx. 1 hour
Calories p. portion: 167
4 portions
Allergens: ACGL

Quantity of ingredients:
Lemon peel 1/2 teaspoon / 2g. (yes)
Ginger fresh 1/2 teaspoon / 2g. (yes)
Basic recipe for a vegetable soup (nutritious) 1 cup / 250g. (yes)
Pepper (ground) 1 pinch / 0,2g. (yes)
Nutmeg 1 pinch / 0,2g. (yes)
Salt 1 pinch / 1g. (little)

Crème fraiche cheese 1 table spoon / 20g. (little)
Basil (fresh) 1 Bunch / 125g. (yes)
Nutmeg 1 pinch / 0,2g. (yes)
Carrot 1/4 lbs - 4oz / 100g. (yes)
Broccoli 1/4 lbs - 4oz / 100g. (yes)
Celery root 1/8 lbs - 2oz / 50g. (yes)
Salt 1 pinch / 1g. (little)
Zucchini 1/4 lbs - 4oz / 100g. (yes)
Potato 5/8 lbs - 8oz / 250g. (yes)
Wheat flour 1 oz / 25g. (yes)
Wheat semolina 1/2 oz / 15g. (yes)
Chicken yolk 1 piece / 20g. (little)
Cauliflower 1/4 lbs - 4oz / 100g. (yes)

Cooking instructions:
Steam the potatoes gently, peel and pass hot through the potato press. Process the hot potatoes with flour, semolina, egg, nutmeg and salt to a smooth dough. Let dough rest for 3o minutes.
Make small rolls (2 cm) out of the dough with flour-dusted hands, cut off 1 cm thin slices. To create the typical gnocchi shape, gently dab the dough pieces with your thumb. Leave the gnocchi in lightly boiling salted water for 6 - 8 minutes. Lift the gnocchi out of the pot with the skimmer.
Heat the vegetable stock till it boils. Add diced celery, grated lemon peel, finely chopped ginger and 1 pinch of nutmeg. Cover and simmer for about 10 minutes. Using the blender, puree the vegetable broth, celery, chopped basil and crème fraiche into a smooth sauce. Season with salt and nutmeg.
Cut carrots, zucchini, cauliflower and broccoli into small pieces and cook covered in a sieve over steam for 8 minutes until firm.
Heat the sauce again and add to the vegetables and arrange over the gnocchi.

9.54 Potato with dandelion salad

Promotes spleen, reduces inflammation, improves digestion, regenerates skin, supports urinating, lowers cholesterol, detoxifying, reduces inflammation, forcing spleen and digestive system, detoxifying, dissolves
Cooking time approx. 25 min
Calories p. portion: 162
2 portions
Allergens:

Quantity of ingredients:
Onion white 1/2 piece / 20g. (yes)
Dandelion (young plants) 1/4 lbs - 4oz / 125g. (yes)
Sunflower oil 1 table spoon / 10g. (yes)
Pepper white (ground) 1 pinch / 0,5g. (yes)
Potato 5/8 lbs - 8oz / 250g. (yes)
Salt 1 pinch / 1g. (little)

Cooking instructions:
Cook the potatoes in salted water and cut into thin slices. Finely chop the onion. Now season the potatoes with oil, salt and pepper and add the dandelion and mix.

9.55 Potato-basil soup

Reduces inflammation, improves digestion, supports urination, lowers cholesterol, reduces blood pressure, strengthens immune system, prevents cancer, reduces radiation damage, antioxidativ, dissolves stagnation.
Cooking time approx. 25 min
Calories p. portion: 96
4 portions
Allergens: L

Quantity of ingredients:
Potato 4 pieces / 200g. (yes)
Sugar cane sugar 1 pinch / 1g. (yes)
Salt 1 pinch / 1g. (little)
Lemon 1 teaspoon / 3g. (yes)
Basil (fresh) 1 Bunch / 50g. (yes)
Ground 1 pinch / 1g. (yes)
Pepper (ground) 1 pinch / 0,5g. (yes)
Carrot 2 pieces / 100g. (yes)
Water 2 cups / 450g. (yes)
Peppers powder 1 pinch / 1g. (yes)
Olive oil 1 table spoon / 10g. (yes)
Garlic 1 clove / 3g. (yes)
Celery root 1 piece / 500g. (yes)

Cooking instructions:
Peeled and chopped 4 medium potatoes in a pot of hot water and 2 chopped medium carrots, a piece of celery root, a pinch of pepper, a pinch of ground cumin, crushed a small clove of garlic, a pinch of salt, 1 teaspoon of lemon juice, simmer until the Vegetables is soft.

Add 1 bunch finely chopped basil into one half of the soup and puree everything; stir in the other half of the basil; with rose paprika, a pinch of whole cane sugar, 1 tablespoon of olive oil or butter, freshly ground pepper, salt to taste.

9.56 Potato bags with wild herbs and tomato sauce

Promotes spleen, reduces inflammation, improves digestion, good to fight loss of appetite, flatulence, inflammatory bowel disease, stimulates liver function, promotes urination, dissolves stagnation, detoxifies, supporting prostate disorders.
Cooking time approx. 45 min
Calories p. portion: 418
5 portions
Allergens: ACG

Quantity of ingredients:
Onion white 1 piece / 50g. (yes)
Pepper (ground) 1 pinch / 0,5g. (yes)
Tomato puree 7/8 lbs / 400g. (yes)
Garlic 1 piece / 2g. (yes)
Garlic 1 piece / 2g. (yes)
Black caraway 1 pinch / 1g. (yes)
Emmental cheese 1/4 lbs / 100g. (little)
Pepper (ground) 1 pinch / 0,5g. (yes)
Salt (herbal) 1/2 teaspoon / 2g. (little)
Chicken egg 1 piece / 60g. (little)
Curd cheese 20% 4 table spoons / 40g. (little)
Salt 1 pinch / 1g. (little)
Olive oil 1 table spoon / 10g. (yes)
Parsley 1/8 lbs - 2oz / 50g. (yes)
Ribworttea 1/2 oz / 10g. (yes)
Chervil dried 1/2 oz / 10g. (yes)
Dandelion (young plants) 1 oz / 30g. (yes)
Nettles 1/8 lbs - 2oz / 50g. (yes)

Nutmeg 1 pinch / 0,2g. (yes)
Pepper (ground) 1 pinch / 0,5g. (yes)
Salt 1 pinch / 1g. (little)
Olive oil 1 table spoon / 10g. (yes)
Cream, sweet 30% 1 table spoon / 10g. (little)
Yarrow 1 oz / 30g. (yes)
Mayonnaise 50% 1 table spoon / 10g. (little)
Wheat flour 5/8 oz / 200g. (yes)
Potato 1,4 lbs / 650g. (yes)

Cooking instructions:
Tomato sauce:
Heat oil. Roast diced onion briefly with crushed garlic. Add the tomato
puree and let it thicken for 2 minutes while stirring, season with salt and
pepper and add the cream and place in a fireproof mold.

Potato Batter:
Cook the boiled potato, drain, peel and squeeze. Mix in a bowl with
flour, Parmesan, egg and spices. Roll out the dough on a lightly floured
work surface and cut into 5 cm squares.

Herb Stuffing:
Chop the herbs and mix with oil, garlic, curd cheese, mayonnaise, herb
salt, crushed black cumin and pepper to a creamy mass.

Put on the pastry with a spoon in the middle. Fold into a triangle, press
on the edge and let the pockets soak in plenty of salted water until they
float up. Add to the tomatoes, sprinkle with the grated cheese and bake
in the oven until golden brown.

9.57 Pumpkin dumplings with tomato and parsley sauce

Protects the digestive system. Good to fight loss of appetite, flatulence,
calms nerves and stomach, helps to digest fat, reduces blood pressure,
stimulates liver function, dissolves stagnation.
Cooking time approx. 30 min
Calories p. portion: 380
2 portions
Allergens: ACG

Quantity of ingredients:
Tomato 1/4 lbs - 4oz / 100g. (yes)
Hokkaido pumpkin 1/4 lbs - 4oz / 100g. (yes)
Chicken egg 2 pieces / 120g. (little)
Wheat flour 1/2-1/3 cup / 120g. (yes)
Pepper (ground) 1 pinch / 0,5g. (yes)
Parmesan 2 table spoons / 20g. (little)
Onion (spring onion) 2 pieces / 40g. (yes)
Parsley 1/2 bunch / 50g. (yes)
Salt 1 pinch / 1g. (little)
Salt 1 pinch / 1g. (little)
Lemon peel 1/2 teaspoon / 2g. (yes)
Nutmeg 1 pinch / 0,2g. (yes)

Cooking instructions:
Peel the pumpkin with a sharp knife, remove the seeds and cut the pulp into large cubes. Wrap pumpkin in aluminum foil, bake in preheated oven at 200°C/392°F for 20 minutes. Pour off any spilled pumpkin juice. Finely crush the pumpkin with the fork. Stir pumpkin and egg until smooth. Stir in so much flour until a dough is formed, from which dumplings can be cut off. Season the mixture with lemon zest, salt, pepper and nutmeg.
Cut off small dumplings with a teaspoon. Leave pumpkin dumplings in boiling salted water for approx. 7 minutes.

Roast the onion in a frying pan until lightly fry the tomato cubes, salt and the chopped parsley.

Arrange pumpkin dumplings in portions with the tomato parsley sauce. Parmesan to hand.

9.58 Pumpkin soup

Promotes digestion, forcing spleen and stomach, reduces blood pressure, strengthens immune system, prevents cancer, reduces radiation damage, improves digestion, regenerates skin, lowers cholesterol, reduces blood glucose, protects liver.
Cooking time approx. 1 hour
Calories p. portion: 105
3 portions
Allergens:

Quantity of ingredients:
Potato 2 pieces / 120g. (yes)
Olive oil 1 table spoon / 10g. (yes)
Pumpkin 3/4 lbs / 300g. (yes)
Carrot 2 pieces / 100g. (yes)
Onion white 1 piece / 50g. (yes)
Water 1 cup / 120g. (yes)
Parsley 1 table spoon / 7g. (yes)
Anise (Common Fennel) 1 pinch / 1g. (yes)
Salt 1 pinch / 1g. (little)

Cooking instructions:
Add the olive oil to the pan, add the diced pumpkin, diced carrots and potatoes. Roast them shortly, add the finely chopped onion, fill with water, add enough water to cover the vegetables at least 3 finger-widths. Boil at low heat.

Season with sea salt, add small cutted parsley, a pinch of anise (little).

Allow to simmer for about 35 minutes. Then purée the soup and add some water, depending on the consistency of the soup.

9.59 Pumpkin-yoghurt soup

Relaxes, reduces blood pressure, strengthens immune system, promotes weight loss. Good to fight immunodeficiency, loss of appetite, flatulence, depressions, diabetes, diarrhea.
Cooking time approx. 15 min
Calories p. portion: 68
4 portions
Allergens: GL

Quantity of ingredients:
Basic recipe for a vegetable soup (nutritious) 1 cup / 300g. (yes)
Salt 1 pinch / 1g. (little)
Peppermint 2 leaves / 1g. (yes)
Yogurt (natural, 1.5% fat) 3/8 lbs - 6oz / 150g. (yes)
Hokkaido pumpkin 1,1 lbs / 500g. (yes)
Anise (Common Fennel) 1/4 teaspoon / 1g. (yes)
Ginger fresh 1/2 teaspoon / 2g. (yes)
Fennel seeds ground 1/2 teaspoon / 1g. (yes)

Cooking instructions:
Heat the vegetable broth (after the basic recipe) till it boils . Add diced pumpkin, chopped ginger, crushed fennel seeds and anise. Bring the soup to the boil and simmer for about 12 minutes until the pumpkin is soft.
Remove soup from the heat. Puree the soup with the yoghurt with the blender. Serve soup with finely chopped mint sprinkled.

9.60 Quick zucchini soup

Diuretic, supports urination. Strengthens gastrointestinal function, expands blood vessels, prevents cancer, prevents diseases (in the elderly). Stimulates liver function, detoxifying.
Cooking time approx. 10 min
Calories p. portion: 42
4 portions
Allergens:

Quantity of ingredients:
Parsley 1 table spoon / 7g. (yes)
Corn germ oil 2 table spoons / 6g. (yes)
Onion white 1 piece / 50g. (yes)
Zucchini 2-3 pieces / 500g. (yes)
Chives 1 teaspoon / 3g. (yes)
Water 2 cup / 400g. (yes)

Cooking instructions:
Fry chopped onion in oil. Add sliced zucchini and sauté well. Pour with water. Chop parsley and chives, add and puree everything.

9.61 Refreshing cucumber soup with potatoes

Diuretic, detoxifying, suppresses conversion of sugar into fat, lowers cholesterol, prevents cancer, reduces inflammation, improves digestion, lowers cholesterol, dissolves stagnation, improves blood circulation, stimulates appetite.
Cooking time approx. 15 min
Calories p. portion: 148
3 portions
Allergens: GN

Quantity of ingredients:
Lemon 1/2 piece / 25g. (yes)
Onion (spring onion) 3 pieces / 60g. (yes)
Pepper (ground) 1 pinch / 0,5g. (yes)
Cream, sweet 30% 1 table spoon / 10g. (little)
Nutmeg 1 pinch / 1g. (yes)
Salt 1 pinch / 1g. (little)
Sesame oil 1 table spoon / 10g. (yes)
Dill 1 table spoon / 15g. (yes)
Potato 4 pieces / 300g. (yes)
Cucumber 2 pieces / 500g. (yes)

Cooking instructions:
Sauté sesame oil, chopped potatoes, plenty of spring onions in a hot pot; add pepper, a little nutmeg, salt, lemon juice, hot water, diced cucumber; simmer for about 10 minutes and then puree; add some sweet cream as you like, fresh dill.

Variation: Add a little chili, oregano, thyme or rosemary to soften the cooling effect.

9.62 Rice congee with carrots and fennel

Worms, forcing spleen, relieves constipation, stimulates nerves, detoxifying, reduces inflammation, improves blood circulation, reduces blood pressure, strengthens immune system, prevents cancer, reduces radiation
Cooking time approx. 2 hours and more
Calories p. portion: 131
3 portions
Allergens: G

Quantity of ingredients:
Cardamom 1/2 teaspoon / 1g. (yes)
Butter Bio 1 teaspoon / 3g. (little)
Carrot 2 pieces / 100g. (yes)
Basic recipe for a rice soup (Congee) 2 cup / 500g. (little)
Fennel 1 piece / 250g. (yes)

Cooking instructions:
Cook rice congee according to basic recipe.
Clean and cut carrots and fennel.

Note:
When carrots and fennel are cooked from the beginning, they serve wholesomeness. If added shortly before the end of the cooking time, taste and vitamins are retained.
Refine with butter and cardamom before serving.

9.63 Rice congee with honey pear and black sesame

Promotes digestion, supports urination, good to fight blood circulation disorders, thromboses, risk of embolism, high blood pressure, a headache, heart attack and stroke.
Cooking time approx. 10 min - 3 hours
Calories p. portion: 158
2 portions
Allergens: N

Quantity of ingredients:
Sesame, black 1 teaspoon / 3g. (yes)
Basic recipe for a rice soup (Congee) 1 1/2 cups / 240g. (little)
Pear 2 pieces / 300g. (yes)

Cooking instructions:
Cook rice congee according to basic recipe.
Fill pot with 3 cm of water and heat till it boils. Quarter the pears (with the skin and seeds) and simmer them covered with black sesame for 10 minutes. Mix with the rice.

9.64 Rice with parsnips

Rich in vitamins, minerals potassium and zinc. Good to fight blood circulation disorders, thrombose, risk of embolism, high blood pressure, a headache, heart attack and stroke, yeast infections.
Cooking time approx. 45 min
Calories p. portion: 206
3 portions
Allergens:

Quantity of ingredients:
Olive oil 1 table spoon / 10g. (yes)
Water 1 1/2 cups / 200g. (yes)
Salt 1 pinch / 1g. (little)
Parsnip 3-4 pieces / 450g. (yes)
Rice variety any 1 cup / 120g. (yes)
Sage 1 teaspoon / 3g. (yes)

Cooking instructions:
Peel the parsnips and cut into slices. Fry for a short time in oil. Add the rice and fry again for a short time. Add the water and cook it at least 30 min. Sprinkle with fresh chopped sage.

9.65 Rice with stewed vegetables

Reduces blood pressure, strengthens immune system, prevents cancer, reduces radiation damage, extremely low fat content, good to fight blood circulation disorders, thrombose, risk of embolism, a headache, heart attack and stroke. Is diuretic.
Cooking time approx. 20 min
Calories p. portion: 166
2 portions
Allergens: L

Quantity of ingredients:
Linseed oil 1 dash / 3g. (yes)
Rice variety any 1/2 cup / 60g. (yes)
Water 1/2 cup / 0g. (yes)
Carrot 2 pieces / 180g. (yes)
Lemon peel 1 piece / 3g. (yes)
Water 3 cups / 300g. (yes)
Celery sticks 1/2 piece / 5g. (yes)
Champignon 1/2 cup / 50g. (yes)
Cress 2 table spoons / 20g. (yes)

Cooking instructions:
Cook rice according to basic recipe with a piece of lemon peel. Steam chopped carrots, celery and mushrooms until soft. Then sprinkle with cress. Then add a dash of high quality cold oil.

9.66 Roasted millet with Celery sticks

Promotes spleen and kidney, diuretic, promoting metabolism.
Cooking time approx. 30 min
Calories p. portion: 400
2 portions
Allergens: L

Quantity of ingredients:
Celery sticks 2 rods / 50g. (yes)
Cress 1 teaspoon / 3g. (yes)

Water 2 table spoons / 30g. (yes)
Millet 1 cup / 120g. (yes)
Water 1 1/2 cups / 240g. (yes)
Sage 3-4 leaves / 2g. (yes)
Herbs various 1 table spoon / 10g. (yes)
Salt 1 pinch / 1g. (little)

Cooking instructions:
Roast millet briefly, pour over water, heat till it boils and let stand for 20 min. to swell.

Cut celery into small pieces and mix with water, salt and fresh herbs and cook for 10 min. Add to the millet.
Sprinkle fresh sage or watercress over it.

9.67 Roasted millet with plum compote

Supports urination, promotes spleen and kidney, strengthens the defense. Good to fight fungi infections.
Cooking time approx. 30 min
Calories p. portion: 139
4 portions
Allergens:

Quantity of ingredients:
Water 1 1/2 cups / 250g. (yes)
Water 5/8 lbs - 8oz / 250g. (yes)
Plum 1 1/2 cups / 250g. (yes)
Cinnamon ground 1 pinch / 1g. (yes)
Millet 1 cup / 120g. (yes)
Acerola fruit nectar or powder 1/2 teaspoon / 1g. (yes)
Vanilla pod 1 pinch / 1g. (yes)

Cooking instructions:
Roast millet briefly, pour over water, heat till it boils and let stand for 20 min. to swell.

Cook plums with water, vanilla and cinnamon 10 min. then strain. Add acerola and add to the millet.

9.68 Rosemary Potatoes

Reduces Inflammation, improves digestion, regenerates skin, supports urination, lowers cholesterol. Rosemary stimulates digestion, strengthens lung, promotes spleen and kidney, dries out.
Cooking time approx. 30 min
Calories p. portion: 188
2 portions
Allergens:

Quantity of ingredients:
Salt (herbal) 1 pinch / 1g. (little)
Rosemary 1 teaspoon / 2g. (yes)
Potato 6-8 pieces / 420g. (yes)
Olive oil 1 table spoon / 10g. (yes)

Cooking instructions:
Cut the potatoes into half's, apply a little olive oil on the cut surface, then salt, sprinkle 2 - 3 rosemary needles on the potatoes.
Place the potatoes on the baking tray and bake them in the preheated oven for approx. 25 minutes to 190°C/374°F.

9.69 Russian kasha with white cabbage

Promotes digestion, relieves pain, detoxifying, promotes digestion, stimulates appetite, dissolves stagnation, stimulates blood production and metabolism, reduces fat.
Cooking time approx. 30 min
Calories p. portion: 250
2 portions
Allergens: AG

Quantity of ingredients:
Butter Bio 1 teaspoon / 3g. (little)
Buckwheat whole grain 1 cup / 130g. (yes)
Salt 1 pinch / 1g. (little)
White cabbage Handful / 20g. (yes)
Parsley 1 table spoon / 10g. (yes)
Water 1 1/2 cups / 240g. (yes)
Nutmeg 1 pinch / 1g. (yes)
Ground 1 pinch / 2g. (yes)

Cooking instructions:
Roast buckwheat golden yellow; add boiling water, heat till it boils briefly and then let it swell until soft; Grate the white cabbage finely and fold in. Season with nutmeg, a little salt; some parsley, cumin and butter at the end.

9.70 Semolina porridge with banana

Regulates gastrointestinal function, reduces inflammation, antiallergic, good to fight blood circulation disorders.
Cooking time approx. 15 min
Calories p. portion: 307
1 portions
Allergens: AG

Quantity of ingredients:
Banana 1/2 piece / 50g. (yes)
Butter Bio 1 teaspoon / 4g. (little)
Spelled semolina 2 table spoons / 30g. (yes)
Cow's milk (whole milk 3.5% fat) 3/4 cup - 6 oz / 200g. (yes)

Cooking instructions:
Heat the half of the milk in a small pot. Add the semolina and boil it shortly in the milk. Let it swell at low heat for 3 minutes with constant stirring. Remove the pot from the heat, add the remaining milk with the snow bean and place the mush in a small bowl. Add the butter and the battered banana.
For adults, a pinch of cinnamon can be spread over it.

9.71 Semolina soup with vegetables

Reduces blood pressure, strengthens immune system, prevents cancer, forcing spleen, dissolves stagnation, promotes weight loss. Good to fight immunodeficiency, loss of appetite, flatulence, high blood pressure, depressions, diabetes, diarrhea, rheumatism, heartburn, twelffinger intestinal ulcers.
Cooking time approx. 20 min
Calories p. portion: 105
3 portions
Allergens: AGL

Quantity of ingredients:
Basil (fresh) 1/2 teaspoon / 1g. (yes)
Lovage 1/2 teaspoon / 2g. (yes)
Wheat semolina 2 table spoons / 20g. (yes)
Basic recipe for a vegetable soup (nutritious) 2 cup / 500g. (yes)
Parsley 1 table spoon / 10g. (yes)
Cream, sweet 30% 2 table spoons / 30g. (little)
Celery root 1/8 lbs - 2oz / 50g. (yes)
Carrot 1/4 lbs - 4oz / 100g. (yes)
Nutmeg 1 pinch / 0,1g. (yes)

Cooking instructions:
Roast wheat grits without fat in a pan. Roast the chopped carrots and celery briefly. Add the vegetable soup (Basic recipe for a vegetable soup). Season with lovage, nutmeg and let it 10 min. simmer.
Stir in the cream before serving and garnish with parsley.

9.72 Spelled with fruit and nuts

Stops diarrhea, promotes digestion, appetizing, relieves fatigue, anti-inflammatory (gastrointestinal). Good to fight tumor lesions and leukemia, is antiallergic in food allergies, regulates metabolism, lowers blood glucose and cholesterol.
Cooking time approx. 1 1/2 hours
Calories p. portion: 290
3 portions
Allergens: AH

Quantity of ingredients:
Cardamom 1 pinch / 1g. (yes)
Apricot 1 piece / 200g. (yes)
Salt 1 pinch / 1g. (little)
Cinnamon ground 1 pinch / 1g. (yes)
Peaches 1 piece / 120g. (yes)
Almond puree 1 table spoon / 15g. (yes)
Apple (sweet) 1 piece / 220g. (yes)
Strawberries 1 cup / 120g. (yes)
Water 1 cup / 50g. (yes)
Cocoa 1 pinch / 1g. (little)
Spelled grain 1 cup / 120g. (yes)
Walnuts 1 table spoon / 10g. (little)

Cooking instructions:
Put spelled in hot water and cook.

Then: Give sweet chopped fruit (apples, apricots, peaches) in a little hot water, with a little cinnamon, sauté briefly; ground cardamom and / or coriander, a small pinch of salt, the boiled spelled, berries after season. Put some cocoa and roasted nuts over it.

9.73 Spring salad

Blood-forming, blood detoxifying, diuretic, good to fight stomach discomfort, improves digestion, diarrhea, helps to digest fat, supports urination, reduces blood pressure, detoxifying, reduces inflammation, diuretic.
Cooking time approx. 10 min
Calories p. portion: 162
4 portions
Allergens: AEMN

Quantity of ingredients:
Parsley 1 Bunch / 50g. (yes)
Mustard 1/2 teaspoon / 2g. (yes)
Mung bean sprouting 0,2 lbs / 75g. (yes)
Soy sauce 1 dash / 3g. (little)
Sorrel 3/8 lbs - 6oz / 150g. (yes)
Cress 1/4 lbs - 4oz / 100g. (yes)
Dandelion (young plants) 1/4 lbs - 4oz / 100g. (yes)
Tomato 2 pieces / 100g. (yes)
White bread (wheat bread) 6 slices / 120g. (yes)
Sesame paste (Tahini) 2 table spoons / 16g. (yes)
Chives 1 Bunch / 50g. (yes)

Cooking instructions:
Wash all salad´s, mix and prepare the sauce as follows:
Mix tahini with mustard and balsamic vinegar, tamari, olive oil, chives and half of parsley. Pour the sauce over the salad and sprinkle the remaining parsley just before serving.
Serve with the white bread.

9.74 Strawberry soup with melons

Relieves pain and inflammation in rheumatism. Diuretic, helps to fight constipation.
Cooking time approx. 5 min
Calories p. portion: 87
2 portions
Allergens:

Quantity of ingredients:
Strawberries 3/4 lbs / 300g. (yes)
Cantaloupe 5/8 oz / 200g. (yes)
Lemon peel 1/4 teaspoon / 1g. (yes)
Strawberry Juice 1/3 cup / 70g. (yes)

Cooking instructions:
Puree strawberries (fresh or frozen) and strawberry juice with the blender, mix in a little sugar.
Cut melon pulp into small pieces.
Arrange strawberry soup in portions. Put the melon cubes in the sweet soup.

9.75 Tae from Dandelionroots

Detoxifying, reduces inflammation.
Cooking time approx. 15 min
Calories p. portion: 1
2 portions
Allergens:

Quantity of ingredients:
Water 2 cup / 500g. (yes)
Dandelion (young plants) 2-4 teaspoons / 6g. (yes)

Cooking instructions:
The chopped dandelion is doused with cold water. Heat the whole thing until it boils and cook for a minute. Then let it rest for ten minutes, filter and enjoy ... Sweet to taste with honey.

9.76 Tea from birch leaves

This tea is diuretic and helps to fight kidney problems, gout, also helps with bacterial and inflammatory urinary tract diseases, rheumatic complaints.
Cooking time approx. 10 min
Calories p. portion: 0
4 portions
Allergens:

Quantity of ingredients:
Water 2 cup / 500g. (yes)

Cooking instructions:
Brew birch leaves with boiling water, let stand for 10 minutes, drink 1 cup 3 times a day.

9.77 Tea from elderberry blossom tea

Good, if you have a sore throat, to fight colds, flu, urinary stones, concentration weakness, blackheads, hay fever, rheumatism.
Strengthen the immune system, diaphoretic.
Cooking time approx. 10 min
Calories p. portion: 7
4 portions
Allergens:

Quantity of ingredients:
Elderberry blossom tee 4 teaspoons / 12g. (recommended)
Water 2 cup / 500g. (yes)

Cooking instructions:
Heat the water till it boils and put it aside. Add holligan flowers and 10 min. to let go. Sweet to taste with honey.
Strain when pouring.

9.78 Tea from juniper berry

Promotes digestion, good to fight loss of appetite, diarrhea, dehydrates, muscle rheumatism and pyelonephritis, improves blood circulation.
Cooking time approx. 10 min
Calories p. portion: 10
1 portions
Allergens:

Quantity of ingredients:
Water 1 cup / 125g. (yes)
Juniper berry 1 teaspoon / 3g. (yes)

Cooking instructions:
A teaspoon of dried juniper berries for a cup of tea. Start cold and bring to the boil. Let it sit for 15 minutes, then
strain.
This tea is unsweetened and swallowed, slowly drunk. The amount is enough for one day.

9.79 Tea from wormwood herb

Good to fight general weakness, flatulence, stomach weakness, bad breath, bile complaints, jaundice, kidney weakness, earache, open wounds. Improves circulation, promotes menstruation.
Cooking time approx. 5 min
Calories p. portion: 0
1 portions
Allergens:

Quantity of ingredients:
Wormwood 1 teaspoon / 2g. (little)
Water 1 cup / 120g. (yes)

Cooking instructions:
Take 2 teaspoons of wormwood herb and pour over 250 ml of boiling water. Let it rest for three minutes, then sift it. Drink half an hour before eating.

9.80 Tea mixture against bile ailments

Good to fight bile complaints or kidney weakness. Analgesic and antispasmodic, calming, hormone regulating, appetizing, strengthens stomach and intestines, diuretic, analgesic and antispasmodic.
Cooking time approx. 10 min
Calories p. portion: 0
4 portions
Allergens:

Quantity of ingredients:
Balm 1 teaspoon / 0,4g. (yes)
Agrimony 1/8 oz / 0,4g. (yes)
Hop 1/8 oz / 0,4g. (yes)
Water 2 cups / 500g. (yes)
Wormwood 1/8 oz / 0,4g. (little)
Dyer's broom herb 1/2 oz / 0,4g. (yes)

Cooking instructions:
Add 1 tablespoon of the mixture to 1 cup of boiling water, infuse for 10 minutes, strain, drink ½ cup 4 times a day!

9.81 Thick pea soup

Supports urination, detoxifying, dissolves stagnation, improves blood circulation, strengthens liver and kidney, strengthens immune system.
Cooking time approx. 2-3 hours
Calories p. portion: 123
3 portions
Allergens: AN

Quantity of ingredients:
Parsley 1 stem / 2g. (yes)
Ground 1/2 teaspoon / 1g. (yes)
Ginger fresh 1/2 teaspoon / 1g. (yes)
Onion white 1/2 piece / 25g. (yes)
Oat meal 1 table spoon / 15g. (yes)
Peas, green 3/8 lbs - 6oz / 150g. (yes)
Salt 1 pinch / 1g. (little)
Water 2 1/4 cups / 550g. (yes)
Sesame oil 1 table spoon / 20g. (yes)

Cooking instructions:
Soak dried peas before cooking. Sauté sesame oil, onion, a little oatmeal, ginger and cumin in a hot pot; add the peas and simmer for 2-3 hours; add salt at the end and purée with a blender; garnish with parsley.

9.82 Tomato soup

Promotes digestion, helps to digest fat, supports urination, reduces blood pressure, dissolves stagnation. Contains unsaturated fatty acids, is antioxidativ.
Cooking time approx. 10 min
Calories p. portion: 100
2 portions
Allergens:

Quantity of ingredients:
Pepper (ground) 1 pinch / 0,5g. (yes)
Cinnamon ground 1 pinch / 1g. (yes)
Peppers powder 1 pinch / 1g. (yes)
Basil (fresh) 1 teaspoon / 2g. (yes)
Olive oil 1 table spoon / 15g. (yes)
Tomato 6 pieces / 250g. (yes)
Salt 1 pinch / 1g. (little)
Onion white 1 piece / 60g. (yes)
Water 5/8 lbs - 8oz / 250g. (yes)

Cooking instructions:
Roast the onion in a pot. Salt and spices. Briefly roast. Put washed and quartered tomatoes in the pan. Stir and sauté briefly. Add a quart of water and heat till it boils. Cook for a quarter of an hour and puree.

9.83 Vanilla cream with berries

Weakness, chronic constipation of the intestine, weight loss, laxative, detoxifying, blood detoxifying. Strengthens the defense. Good to fight fungi infections.
Cooking time approx. 15 min
Calories p. portion: 278
4 portions
Allergens: G

Quantity of ingredients:
Acerola fruit nectar or powder 1 teaspoon / 2g. (yes)
Vanilla sugar natural 3 package / 3g. (yes)
Blackberry´s 1/4 lbs - 4oz / 100g. (yes)
Raspberry 1/4 lbs - 4oz / 100g. (yes)
Strawberries 1/4 lbs - 4oz / 100g. (yes)
Cream (30% fat) 1/4 lbs - 4oz / 125g. (little)
Curd cheese 20% 7/8 lbs / 400g. (little)

Yogurt (natural, 1.5% fat) 3/8 lbs - 6oz / 150g. (yes)
Sugar brown 2 teaspoons / 8g. (yes)
Blueberry 1/4 lbs - 4oz / 100g. (yes)

Cooking instructions:
Mix the curd cheese, yoghurt, sugar, acerola and vanilla sugar with a hand mixer or whisk until smooth. Beat the whipped cream very stiff, mix it under the cream. Arrange vanilla cream in portions with the berries.

9.84 Vegetable bowl with Provencal pistou

Promotes spleen and liver, reduces blood pressure, strengthens immune system, prevents cancer, reduces radiation damage, forcing spleen, dissolves stagnation. Relieves constipation, strengthens mother milk
Cooking time approx. 1 1/2 hours
Calories p. portion: 138
8 portions
Allergens: AGL

Quantity of ingredients:
Salt 1 pinch / 2g. (little)
Parmesan 1 oz / 30g. (little)
Basil (fresh) 1 Bunch / 125g. (yes)
Fennel 1 piece / 250g. (yes)
Broccoli 5/8 oz / 200g. (yes)
Potato 1/4 lbs - 4oz / 100g. (yes)
Celery root 1/4 lbs - 4oz / 100g. (yes)
Carrot 3/8 lbs - 6oz / 150g. (yes)
Pepper (ground) 1 pinch / 1g. (yes)
Thyme dried 1/2 teaspoon / 2g. (yes)
Basic recipe for a vegetable soup (nutritious) 3 lbs / 1250g. (yes)
Toast bread (whole grain) 1 slice / 5g. (yes)
Garlic 1 clove / 5g. (yes)
Olive oil 2 table spoons / 30g. (yes)
Tomato 5/8 oz / 200g. (yes)
Oregano dried 1 teaspoon / 3g. (yes)
Onion (spring onion) 4 pieces / 80g. (yes)
Peas, green 1/8 lbs - 2oz / 50g. (yes)
Bay leaf 1 piece / 0,5g. (yes)
Oregano dried 1/2 teaspoon / 2g. (yes)

Cooking instructions:
Sauce:
Tear off tomatoes and cut into small pieces. Reduce in a pot with a little olive oil, finely chopped garlic. Add 1 slice of dry toasted bread (crumbed), fresh finely grated Parmesan, finely chopped basil, oregano, salt and pepper.

Soup:
Boil the vegetable broth according to the basic recipe, add coarsely sliced carrots, diced celery, diced potatoes, small florets, broccoli, finely chopped fennel tuber, peas, thyme, oregano and the bay leaf. let cook 10 minutes.

Cut 4 scallions into thin rings, add them and cook another 2 min.

Pour sauce into a soup bowl. First only a few tablespoons. Stir boiling broth with it, then stir in the soup little by little.

9.85 Vegetable juice

Promotes digestion, helps to digest fat, supports urination, reduces blood pressure, strengthens immune system, prevents cancer, reduces radiation damage, forcing spleen, is stimulating.
Cooking time approx. 15 min
Calories p. portion: 64
1 portions
Allergens: L

Quantity of ingredients:
Tomato 1/4 lbs - 4oz / 100g. (yes)
Acerola fruit nectar or powder 1/2 teaspoon / 1g. (yes)
Garlic 1 piece / 2g. (yes)
Carrot 1/4 lbs - 4oz / 100g. (yes)
Celery root 1/2 oz / 20g. (yes)
Salt 1 teaspoon / 2g. (little)

Cooking instructions:
Peel all ingredients and use the juicer to make a drink. Stir in the acerola.

9.86 Vegetable rice

Forcing spleen, dissolves stagnation, promotes weight loss. Good to fight immunodeficiency, loss of appetite, flatulence, high blood pressure, strengthens kidney and bladder. Diuretic, warming the body from the inside, regulates internal organs functions.
Cooking time approx. 30 min
Calories p. portion: 304
3 portions
Allergens: L

Quantity of ingredients:
Rice (whole grain) 5/8 oz / 200g. (yes)
Pepper (ground) 1 pinch / 0,2g. (yes)
Parsley 1/2 oz / 20g. (yes)
Basic recipe for a vegetable soup (nutritious) 7/8 lbs / 400g. (yes)
Broccoli 1/8 lbs - 2oz / 50g. (yes)
Carrot 1/8 lbs - 2oz / 50g. (yes)
Kohlrabi 1/8 lbs - 2oz / 50g. (yes)
Cauliflower 1 oz / 30g. (yes)
Peas 1/2 oz / 20g. (yes)
Margarine 1 teaspoon / 4g. (little)

Cooking instructions:
Cut the broccoli, carrots and kohlrabi into small cubes, divide the cauliflower into small florets. Heat the margarine in a pan or saucepan, sauté the vegetables. Then add the rice, top up with the vegetable stock and leave to soak for 15-20 minutes.

In the meantime finely chop the parsley. After cooking, season the rice with freshly ground pepper and parsley.

9.87 Vegetable semolina soup

Diuretic, harmonizes the stomach and intestines, conducts bowel winds, reduces blood pressure, lowers cholesterol, detoxifying, good to fight loss of appetite, flatulence, inflammatory bowel disease, heartburn, twelffinger intestinal ulcers. Stimulates digestion, reduces pain.
Cooking time approx. 20 min
Calories p. portion: 199
3 portions
Allergens: AEGL

Quantity of ingredients:
Wheat semolina 2 table spoons / 24g. (yes)
Kohlrabi 1/2 piece / 200g. (yes)
Soy sauce 1 teaspoon / 3g. (little)
Celery root 3/8 lbs - 6oz / 150g. (yes)
Butter Bio 1 table spoon / 20g. (little)
Basic recipe for a vegetable soup (nutritious) 2 cup / 500g. (yes)
Lovage 1/2 teaspoon / 2g. (yes)
Parsnip 1 piece / 180g. (yes)
Carrot 1 piece / 120g. (yes)
Potato 1 piece / 80g. (yes)
Beans (green, fresh) 1/4 lbs / 100g. (yes)

Cooking instructions:
Worm the prepared vegetable soup; cook the vegetables in the soup softly. Spread some wheatgrass and let it swell. At the end, add lovage-green and a little butter and taste with soy sauce.

9.88 Warming carrot soup

Strengthens and warms, reduces blood pressure, strengthens immune system, prevents cancer, reduces radiation damage, strengthens gastrointestinal function.
Cooking time approx. 30 min
Calories p. portion: 133
3 portions
Allergens: HL

Quantity of ingredients:
Carrot 4 pieces / 250g. (yes)
Nutmeg 1 pinch / 1g. (yes)
Ginger fresh 1/2 teaspoon / 1g. (yes)
Salt 1 pinch / 1g. (little)
Parsley 1 table spoon / 10g. (yes)
Basic recipe for a vegetable soup (nutritious) 2 cup / 500g. (yes)
Anise (Common Fennel) 1/2 teaspoon / 1g. (yes)
Onion (shallot) 2 pieces / 40g. (yes)
Walnut oil 2 table spoons / 20g. (yes)

Cooking instructions:
Heat walnut oil in a hot pot and fry onions; steam the carrots in it; add anise, nutmeg, a little ginger, salt and sauté everything; add water or vegetable- or meat stock; cook everything soft and then puree; fold in parsley at the end.

Recommendation: Suitable for the cold season, especially if you use meat broth as a liquid for infusion.

9.89 Wheat semolina with olives-herb-souce and salad

Protects the digestive system. Detoxifying, affects anorexia, good to fight flatulence, inflammatory bowel disease, obesity, gout, stomach ulcers, stomach cramps, rheumatism, heartburn. Dissolves stagnation, relieves
Cooking time approx. 15 min
Calories p. portion: 245
3 portions
Allergens: ACGL

Quantity of ingredients:
Olive oil 1 teaspoon / 3g. (yes)
Lemon peel 1 pinch / 1g. (yes)
Onion white 1 piece / 60g. (yes)
Olive oil 1 teaspoon / 2g. (yes)
Chives 1 table spoon / 7g. (yes)
Pepper (ground) 1 pinch / 0,5g. (yes)
Water 1/3 cup / 65g. (yes)
Oregano fresh 1 teaspoon / 2g. (yes)
Chicken egg 1 piece / 60g. (little)
Wheat semolina 1/4 lbs - 4oz / 100g. (yes)
Basic recipe for a vegetable soup (nutritious) 2 cups / 500g. (yes)
Cream, sweet 30% 1/8 lbs - 2oz / 40g. (little)
Lettuce 2 handful / 30g. (yes)
Lemon juice 1 teaspoon / 3g. (yes)

Cooking instructions:
Mix cream and water and heat till it boils. Stir in the wheat semolina and cook to a thick porridge and remove from heat. Whisk the egg and stir in, season with pepper and grated lemon zest. Form with 2 coffee spoons, dumplings and leave to stir in the slightly boiling vegetable stock until the dumplings float up.
Chop the onion and roast it in olive oil in a pan. Pour the semolina

dumplings into the pan and sprinkle with finely chopped chives.

Wash salad and cut into thin strips. Season with olive oil, lemon juice and oregano.

9.90 Whole milk cereal mash

Reduces Inflammation, antiallergic, has a stabilizing effect on the blood circulation, lowers blood glucose and cholesterol.
Cooking time approx. 20 min
Calories p. portion: 205
1 portions
Allergens: AG

Quantity of ingredients:
Spelled flakes 1/2 oz / 20g. (yes)
Water 1/4 cup / 50g. (yes)
Cow's milk (whole milk 3.5% fat) 3/4 cup - 6 oz / 200g. (yes)
Fruit mix juice 1/2 oz / 20g. (yes)

Cooking instructions:
Boil the milk with the wholegrain flakes and let it swell. Add the pureed fruit.

Switch between wheat, oats and wholemeal spelled flakes, as well as the fruits. So you get a variety of flavors.

9.91 Yellow lentil soup

Strengthens heart and kidney, diuretic, promotes spleen, calms the stomach, promotes digestion, strengthens immune system, prevents cancer, reduces radiation damage, stimulates liver function, antioxidativ.
Cooking time approx. 20 min
Calories p. portion: 155
7 portions
Allergens: A

Quantity of ingredients:
Carrot 2 pieces / 150g. (yes)
Lemon juice 1/2 piece / 15g. (yes)
White bread (wheat bread) 7 slices / 140g. (yes)
Salt 1 pinch / 1g. (little)
Cardamom 1 pinch / 1g. (yes)

Turmeric (yellow root) 1 pinch / 1g. (yes)
Olive oil 1 table spoon / 10g. (yes)
Kohlrabi 1 piece / 300g. (yes)
Onion white 1 piece / 50g. (yes)
Lentils yellow 1 lbs / 500g. (little)
Parsley 1/2 bunch / 100g. (yes)
Water 4 cup / 1000g. (yes)

Cooking instructions:
Wash lenses well in a colander. Heat oil in a pot. Add finely chopped onion, sliced carrots, diced kohlrabi and spices, sauté and salt. Add the lentils and cover with water and simmer for 20 minutes. Add water as needed and season with salt. Sprinkle with fresh parsley or fresh green cilantro and drizzle with lemon juice.
Here you can also use red lenses. (same cooking time).
Serve with white bread.

9.92 Zucchini semolina cream soup

Good to fight loss of appetite, reduces blood pressure, promotes weight loss. Good to fight loss of appetite, flatulence, inflammatory bowel disease, rheumatism, heartburn.
Cooking time approx. 25 min
Calories p. portion: 146
4 portions
Allergens: AGL

Quantity of ingredients:
Salt 1 pinch / 1g. (little)
Parsley 1 Bunch / 100g. (yes)
Wheat semolina 2 table spoons / 20g. (yes)
Basic recipe for a vegetable soup (nutritious) 3 1/2 cups / 800g. (yes)
Lovage 1/2 teaspoon / 2g. (yes)
Nutmeg 1 pinch / 0,5g. (yes)
Anise (Common Fennel) 1 pinch / 0,5g. (yes)
Zucchini 7/8 lbs / 400g. (yes)
Ginger fresh 1/2 teaspoon / 1g. (yes)
Crème fraiche cheese 2 table spoons / 20g. (little)
Lemon peel 1/4 piece / 2g. (yes)
Butter Bio 1/2 oz / 20g. (little)
Pepper (ground) 1 pinch / 0,5g. (yes)

Cooking instructions:
Melt the butter in a saucepan, add the semolina and fry briefly while stirring. Add half of the chopped parsley, sauté for a short time, pour vegetable broth according to the basic recipe, season with chopped lovage, nutmeg and anise. Cook the soup without lid lightly for 10 minutes. Add the finely chopped zucchini and the small piece of lemon zest, cook gently for 5 minutes until the zucchini are tender. Remove the lemon peel.
Using the blender, finely puree the soup with the crème fraiche and the remaining parsley.

10 Effects of food

10.1 Use ingredients: recommendable

Acai powder
Bitter Herb liqueur
Cranberries
Cranberry
Cranberry jam
Cranberry juice
Cream 10% coffee cream
Currant (black)

Currant (red)
Currant (white)
Elderberry blossom tee
Fox nut, gorgon nut, makhana
Hibiscus
Kudzu
Lily bulbs
Mascarpone cheese

10.2 Use ingredients: yes

Acerola fruit nectar or powder
Adzuki beans
Agar agar (kelp)
Agave nectar
Agrimony
Almond
Almond marzipan
Almond milk
Almond puree
Aloe juice
Amaranth
Amaranth Pops
Angelica root
Anise (Common Fennel)
Apple (sour)
Apple (sweet)
Apple juice (natural cloudy)
Apple puree
Apricot
Apricot dried
Apricot jam
Apricot nectar
Apricots
Apricots juice
Arrowroot
Artichoke
Asparagus (green or white)
Aubergine
Avocado
Baking powder
Balm
Bamboo shoots
Banana
Banana (cooking banana)
Banchatee (green tea)
barberry
Barley
Barley flour

Barley grass powder
Barley grouts
Barley malt
Barley not peeled
Basic recipe for a vegetable soup
(nutritious)
Basil
Basil (fresh)
Batavia
Bay leaf
Bean oil
Beans (green, fresh)
Bearberry leaf
Berries of the season
Berry juice
Bitter Lemon
Bitter orange peel
Black caraway
Black fungus mushroom
Blackberry dried (unripe fruit)
Blackberry jam
Blackberry leaves
Blackberry´s
Blackthorn (Sloe)
Blue mallow tee
Blueberry
Blueberry dried
Blueberry jam
Blueberry juice
Bocksdorn fruits (Fructus Lycii, Goji,
goji berry dried
Boletus mushroom
Borage
Borage oil
Boxhorn clover seeds
Bread roll
Bread with carob kernel flour
Breadcrumbs (wheat bread, bread roll)

Broccoli
Brussels sprouts
Buckbean
Buckwheat
Buckwheat (roasted) Kasha
Buckwheat whole grain
Bulgur (cereals)
Burdock root tea
Bush beans
Butter beans white
Cantaloupe
Carambola (Star fruit)
Cardamom
Carob flour, St. john's bread
Carrot
Carrot (Early Carrot)
Carrot juice without sugar
Cauliflower
Celery root
Celery sticks
Cereal coffee
Chamomile
Chamomile tea
Champignon
Channa-Dal
Chanterelle
Chenpi (chinese tangerine bowl)
Cherry
Cherry (sour)
Cherry compote
Cherry juice
Chervil
Chervil dried
Chestnut puree
Chestnuts
Chickpeas
Chickweed
Chicory
Chili (pod or ground)
Chinese cabbage
Chinese pearl barley
Chives
Chlorella (fresh water)
Chrysanthemum blossom tea
Cinnamon ground
Cinnamon sticks
Clementine
Clementines
Clove
Coconut fat
Coconut flakes
Coconut grated
Coconut meat
Coconut milk

Codfish
Coffee
Coix (seeds) YiYi Ren
Compote (fruits of the season)
Coriander
Coriander (fresh)
Corn
Corn (fast polenta)
Corn (roasted)
Corn flour
Corn germ oil
Corn Grease (Polenta)
Corn silk tea
Corn starch
Couscous
Cow's milk (1.5% fat)
Cow's milk (whole milk 3.5% fat)
Cranberry
Cream sour 10%
Creamer
Cress
Crispbread
Crucian
Cucumber
Cucumber (bitter)
Cucumber (spicy cucumber)
Cumin (Caraway seed)
Curcuma
Currant jam (black)
Currant jam (red)
Currant juice (black)
Currants (black)
Currants (red)
Curry
Curry paste red
Daisy
Dandelion (young plants)
Dandelion juice
Dandelionroots tea
Dashi
Dates dried
Dates red
Dill
Ducks egg
Dulse (seaweed)
Dyer's broom herb
Elderberries
Endive salad
Evening primrose oil
Fennel
Fennel seeds ground
Fennel tea
Fenugreek (Trigonella foenum-graecum)

Fig
Fig dried
Fish pieces mixed (fresh water)
Flounder
Flower pollen
Fresh cheese from soya
Fructose (glucose)
Fruit mix juice
Fruit tea
Gail plum
Galangal
Garam Masala powder
Garlic
Gelee Royal
Gentian root
Gentian root tea
Ginger fresh
Ginger oil
Ginger powder
Ginkgo fruit
Ginseng
Ginseng root
Gooseberry
Gourd
Grape juice red
Grape juice white
Grapefruit (Pomelo)
Grapefruit dried peel
Grapefruit juice
Grapes red
Grapes white
Grapeseed oil
Grass carp
Green spelt
Greengage
Ground
Ground caraway
Guava
Hawthorn
Herbal tea mix
Herbs bitter
Herbs of Provence
Herbs various
Herbs wild
Hibiscus tea
Hijiki
Hokkaido pumpkin
Honey
Hop
Horehound leaves
Hyssop
Iceberg lettuce
Jasmine blossoms tee
Juniper berry

Kaki plum
Kalmus
King Solomon's-seal
Kiwi
Kohlrabi
Kombu seaweed (Saccharina japonica)
Kukicha tea
Kumquats
Lamb's lettuce
Lamb's lettuce
Lavender blossoms
Leaf salads (bitter)
Leek
Lemon
Lemon Balm (dried)
Lemon Balm (fresh)
Lemon juice
Lemon peel
Lemongrass
Lettuce
Licorice root tea
Lima beans
Lime
Lime blossom tea
Linseed
Linseed (crushed)
Linseed oil
Liver smoothing tea
Longane
Loquate / Japanese medlar
Lotus roots
Lotus seeds
Lovage
Lovage seeds
Luo Han Guo fruit
Lychee
Lye roll
Mallow (Malva sylvestris) blossom tea
Malt
Mango
Mango juice
Manioc flour
Maple syrup
Mare's milk
Marjoram
Millet
Millet flakes
Mirabelle plum
Mixed Pickles
Morel (black, dried)
Morel, dried
Mu Erh Mushroom
Muesli
Mulberry fruit

Mulled Wine Spice
Mullet
Multi-grain bread (gray bread)
Mung bean
Mung bean sprouting
Mustard
Mustard Dijon
Mustard medium hot
Mustard seeds
Mustard sweet
Nasturtium (nose-twister or nose-tweaker)
Nectarine
Nettles
Noodles (wheat) with egg
Noodles (wheat, lasagne) with egg
Noodles (wheat, ribbon noodles) with egg
Noodles (wheat, spaghetti) with egg
Noodles (whole grain) with egg
Nori, purple seaweed, red algae
Nutmeg
Oat
Oat flakes (whole grain)
Oat flakes roasted
Oat flour
Oat fusion (baby food)
Oat meal
Oat milk
Okra
Olive oil
Olives
Olives green
Onion (shallot)
Onion (spring onion)
Onion read
Onion white
Orange
Orange blossom
Orange dried peel
Orange grated peel
Orange jam
Orange juice
Orange peel
Oregano dried
Oregano fresh
Oyster mushroom
Oyster shell powder
Oysters
Palm oil
Papaya
Parsley
Parsley root
Parsnip

Passion blossoms tea
Passion fruit
Peaches
Peaches (canned)
Pear
Pear juice
Pearl barley
Pearl barley
Peas
Peas, green
Pepper (ground)
Pepper Cayenne
Pepper powder (hot)
Pepper white (ground)
Peppercorns
Peppermint
Peppermint tea
Pepperoni
Pepperoni, red, pitted, halved
Pepperoni, yellow, pitted, halved
Peppers
Peppers (rose peppers)
Peppers (sweet)
Peppers powder
Perch
Pickle
Pimento
Pine nuts
Pineapple
Pineapple juice without sugar
Pinto beans speckled
Pistachios
Plaice
Plum
Plum dried
Plums
Pomegranate
Poppy
Potato
Potato (mealy)
Potato flour
Prickly pear
Psyllium seed
Pudding powder vanilla
Puff pastry
Pumpernickel (dark bread)
Pumpkin
Pumpkin seed oil
Pumpkin seeds
Quince
Quinoa
Radicchio
Radish
Radish (white, green, purple-red)

Radish black
Radish horseradish
Radish leaves
Raisins
Rapeseed oil
Raspberry
Raspberry dried (immature)
Raspberry jam
Raspberry leaf tea
Red berry (without sugar)
Red cabbage
Reishi mushroom
Ribwort tea
Rice (fragrance)
Rice (Gaoliang / Sorghum)
Rice (whole grain)
Rice Basmati
Rice black
Rice flour
Rice long grain rice
Rice malt
Rice mash
Rice noodles
Rice red
Rice round grain
Rice starch
Rice sticky
Rice sweet
Rice variety any
Rice wild (nature rice)
Romaine lettuce / lettuce salad
Rose blossom tea
Rose hip
Rose hip tea
Rose leaf tea
Rosemary
Rucola
Rusk
Rye
Rye flour
Rye wholemeal bread
Safflower (Dyer's thistle / Hong Hua)
Saffron
Sage
Sago (cereals)
Sake
Salmon
Salsify
Sauerkraut (cutted cabbage fermented)
Savory
Savoy cabbage / kale
Sea buckthorn
Sea cucumber
Sesame oil

Sesame oil roasted
Sesame paste (Tahini)
Sesame, black
Sesame, white
Shiitake, dried
Skim milk powder
Slug
Sorrel
Sour cherries
Sour cream 15% fat
Sour milk
Sourdough
Spelled (Dark) bread
Spelled flakes
Spelled grain
Spelled semolina
Spelled wholemeal flour
Spurdog (spiny dogfish, Schillerlocken)
St. Benedict's thistle, blessed thistle,
holy thistle, spotted thistle
Star anise
Stevia (candyleaf, sweetleaf)
Strawberries
Strawberry jam
Strawberry Juice
Sugar - icing sugar
Sugar brown
Sugar candy white
Sugar cane sugar
Sugar fructose - fruit sugar
Sugar glucose - grapes sugar
Sugar Milk Sugar
Sugar molasses
Sugar palm sugar
Sugar substitute (sweetener)
Sugar white
Sunflower oil
Sunflower seeds
Sweet potato
Tabasco
Tangerine
Tarragon (Estragon)
Tea mixture uric acid lowering
Thistle oil
Thyme
Thyme dried
Toast bread (whole grain)
Tomato
Tomato dried
Tomato juice
Tomato paste
Tomato puree
Tonic Water
Topinambur

Trout
Truffle
Tsampa (roasted barley flour)
Turmeric (yellow root)
Turnips
Umeboshi paste
Umeboshi plums (Japanese apricots)
Valerian
Vanilla
Vanilla pod
Vanilla powder
Vanilla sugar natural
Vegetable juice
Vinegar (Apple vinegar)
Vinegar (Red wine vinegar)
Vinegar Aceto Balsamico
Vinegar Aceto Balsamico white
Wakame
Walnut oil
Water
Water hot
Watermelon
Wax gourd
Wheat
Wheat bran
Wheat bulgur
Wheat flakes
Wheat flatbread/pita bread
Wheat flour
Wheat flour whole grain
Wheat germ oil

Wheat semolina
Wheat semolina for children
Wheat/Rye/Gray-black bread with yeast
Wheatgrass juice
Wheatgrass powder
Whey
White bread (baguette)
White bread (pretzel sticks)
White bread (roll)
White bread (wheat bread)
White breadcrumbs
White cabbage
White dumpling bread (wheat bread cut into chunks)
Whitefish
Whole grain bread
Wholemeal flour
Wild garlic (garlic spinach)
Wild herbs
Wild strawberries
Wormwood herb
Yam root, yam root tuber
Yarrow
Yarrow tea
Yeast
Yoghurt vanilla
Yogi tea
Yogurt (natural, 1.5% fat)
Yogurt (natural, 3.5% fat)
Zucchini

10.3 Use ingredients: little

Anchovy / Sardine
Basic recipe for a beef soup
Basic recipe for a beef soup (warming)
Basic recipe for a chicken soup (warming)
Basic recipe for a duck soup
Basic recipe for a fish soup
Basic recipe for a rice soup (Congee)
Beef bone marrow
Beef fillet
Beef heart
Beef heart (calf)
Beef kidney
Beef liver
Beef lungs (calf)
Beef meat
Beef meat (calf)
Beef meatbones
Beef Oxtail pieces

Beef soup meat
Beef stomach
Black beans
Black-eyed peas
Brazil nuts
Brie cheese
Broad beans (thick beans)
Brown ale
Butter (half fat)
Butter Bio
Buttermilk
Calamari
Camembert
Capers in olive oil
Carp
Cashews
Caviar
Chicken Blood
Chicken egg

Chicken egg white
Chicken heart
Chicken liver
Chicken meat
Chicken stomach
Chicken yolk
Chocolate
Chocolate (Diabetic)
Cocoa
Cod
Cola drink
Cola drink (low calorie)
Cooking oil
Cottage cheese
Crab
Cream (30% fat)
Cream sour 20%
Cream sour 30%
Cream, sweet 30%
Crème fraiche cheese
Curd cheese 20%
Curd cheese 40%
Deer meat
Deer meat
Deer's Bones
Deer's kidneys
Duck (heart)
Duck (slaughtered)
Edam cheese
Eel
Eel smoked
Emmental cheese
Fernet Branca (herbal bitter liqueur)
Feta cheese
Feta cheese
Fish innards
Fish remains
Fish sauce
French beans
Fresh cheese
Fresh cheese with herbs
Freshwater crab
Freshwater fish
Gelatin white
Ginseng liqueur
Goat
Goat and sheep's blood
Goat and sheep's brain
Goat and sheep's liver
Goat and sheep's milk
Goat and sheep's stomach
Goat cheese
Goose
Goose blood

Goose egg
Goose fat
Goose parts
Gorgonzola
Gouda cheese
Halibut (Flatfish)
Hazelnuts
Herring
Honey wine (Met)
Horse meat
Jellyfish
Kefir
Kidney beans (red)
Ladyfingers
Lamb bones
Lamb kidneys
Lamb liver
Lamb meat
Lamb shoulder
Lentils
Lentils black
Lentils red
Lentils yellow
Lobster
Lychee in Preserved
Lychee liqueur
Mackerel
Margarine
Margarine (diet)
Martini
Mayonnaise 50%
Mayonnaise 80%
Mediterranean fish (cod, plaice,
haddock, sea eel, mackerel)
Medlar
Mineral water
Miso
Miso black (fermented)
Miso paste (soy bean paste)
Mold cheese
Mozzarella
Mussels
Mutton
Mutton
Octopus
Octopus
Parmesan
Peanut (roasted)
Peanut oil
Pheasant
Pig blood
Pigeon
Pigeon egg
Pineapple (from a can)

Pork Bacon
Pork brain
Pork fat (lard)
Pork ham
Pork ham cooked
Pork ham smoked
Pork heart
Pork kidneys
Pork knuckle
Pork Lard
Pork liver
Pork lung
Pork marrow bones
Pork meat
Pork sausage (Bratwurst)
Pork skin
Pork stomach
Pork/beef sausage (smoked)
Pork's intestine
Processed cheese 12%
processed cheese 30%
Prosecco
Quail
Quail egg
Rabbit
Rabbit (wild)
Rabbit liver
Rabbit meat
Rosefish
Rum
Salt
Salt (herbal)
Seacrab
Shark

Sheep's milk
Sheep's milk yoghurt
Sherry (whine)
Shrimp
Shrimps
Sour milk cheese 20%
Soy flour
Soy noodles
Soy sauce
Soy Tofu
Soy Tofu smoked
Soya Cuisine (soy cream)
Soybean milk
Soybean oil
Soybeans
Soybeans, black
Soybeans, blacks, fermented
Soybeans, yellow
Spiny lobsters
Spirit
Trout (smoked)
Tuna
Turkey breast meat
Turkey ham
Turnip
Walnuts
Walnuts roasted
Wheat beer
White beans
White wine
Wild boar meat
Wormwood
Yew nut

10.4 Do not use contra-acting foods

Beer (alcohol-free)
Beer (alcohol-reduced)
Beer (Pils)
Beer (Top-fermented German dark
beer)
Bitter liqueur
Black tea
Campari
Chard

Clarified butter
Green tea
Peanut butter
Peanuts
Red beet
Red wine
Rhubarb
Spinach
Supplementary nutrition

11 Herbs and their effects

11.1 Basil (fresh)

It has a beneficial effect on flatulence and nausea, relaxing and soothing. Good to fight emphysema, bronchitis, whooping cough, high blood pressure, headache, mouth odor, warts, hiccup, gout, migraine.

11.2 Birch leaves

This tea is diuretic and helps to fight kidney ailments, gout and cleans the blood, also helps with bacterial and inflammatory urinary tract diseases, kidney grief and rheumatic complaints.

11.3 Nettles

Promotes urination. Tea or juice, cleanses the blood and the kidneys, supports prostate problems, inhibit the formation of inflammation, pain-relieving.

11.4 Dill

The medicinal and spice herb has an antispasmodic effect and stimulates gastric juice production. Good to fight flatulence. Antispasmodic for gastrointestinal discomfort.

11.5 Dyer's broom herb

The Herb is used as a diuretic (for the purge of water) and for digestion. Due to the side effects, birch leaves or dandelions are recommended rather than the Dyer broom, which have very similar effects, but are not toxic.

11.6 Hop

Calming, hormone-regulating, appetizing, strengthens the stomach and intestines, diuretic, pain-relieving and antispasmodic.

11.7 Chervil dried

Forces urination, detoxifying, blood-purifying and blood-pressure-reducing effects.

11.8 Coriander

The essential oils are appetizing, digestive, cramping and soothing in stomach and intestinal disorders.

11.9 Herbs various

Appetizing, lots of trace elements and vitamins

11.10 Cress

Diuretic, supports urination. Good to fight dry mouth, inner agitation, sore throat, diabetes, kidney stones, gastrointestinal complaints, lung problems, menstrual cramps or cancer.

11.11 Chives

Bactericide, prevents cancer, strengthens gastric juice production, promotes digestion and blood circulation, promotes growth, triggers stagnation.

11.12 Lovage

Stimulates digestion, reduces pain. Extracts of the root are used to flush out urinary tract infections and prevent kidney gravel.

11.13 Dandelion (young plants)

Detoxifies, relieves inflammation. Regulates digestion, helps with rheumatism, releases kidney stones, leaves pimples and chronic skin disorders disappear.

11.14 Balm

Soothing effect, Good for insomnia, restlessness and upset stomach, Allergies, Asthma, Migraine, Flatulence, Headache, Rheumatism and mental tension. To strengthen after cold and infectious diseases.

11.15 Agrimony

Good to fight persistent rheumatism, bedwetting, some mouth sores and spleen disease. For the treatment of wounds and inflammations of the skin as envelopes.

11.16 Oregano fresh

It has an anti-digestive, calming and nerve-strengthening effect, helps to fight cramping stomach and intestinal disorders. The ingredient Carvacrol has an anti-inflammatory effect.

11.17 Oregano dried

It has an anti-digestive, calming and nerve-strengthening effect, helps to fight cramping stomach and intestinal disorders. The ingredient Carvacrol has an anti-inflammatory effect.

11.18 Parsley

Stimulates liver function, detoxifies. Forces urinating. Relieves flatulence. Digestive and menstrual stimulating, birth-accelerating, memory-enhancing, blood-purifying, skin-smoothing.

11.19 Peppermint

Relaxes, frees the lungs and the nose (inhale), regulates the cycle. Stimulates bile flow and bile production, antispasmodic in gastrointestinal disorders, antimicrobial and antiviral.

11.20 Rosemary

Promotes digestion, relieves bloating, strengthens lung, spleen and kidney. Affects the circulation and nerves. Appetizing. Baths help to fight circulatory disorders as well as with gout and rheumatism.

11.21 Sage

Good to fight yeast infections. The leaves have a digestive effect and are used in greasy foods. Antiperspirant effect. Helps to relieve coughing attacks. Dries out (TCM).

11.22 Sorrel

Astringent, hematopoietic, purifies the blood, diuretic. Good to fight liver weakness, upset stomach, indigestion, constipation, diarrhea, worms, scurvy, anemia, women's complaints, wounds, skin rashes, boils, ulcers, swelling.

11.23 Black caraway

Detoxifying, immunoregulatory. In addition, the oil should stimulate the formation of bone marrow cells and generally protect body cells from viruses.

11.24 Thyme dried

Disinfecting. It stimulates the blood circulation, increases the appetite and helps to digest fat meat better. Strengthens lungs and spleen (TCM).

11.25 Lemongrass

Reduction of flatulence, antimicrobial, appetizing. Prevention of influenza. Good to fight infections in the mouth and throat.

11.26 Lemon Balm (fresh)

Stimulating, antibacterial, encouraging, relaxing, antispasmodic, cooling, antipyretic, analgesic, sweat-inducing, virus-inhibiting. Good for colds, fever, flu, cough, bronchitis, asthma, loss of appetite, bloating, heartburn.

12 Basics of Nutrition

The basic principles of nutrition described herein are general recommendations. They are not aimed at a specific form of therapy. Recommendations concerning a therapy have priority.

12.1 Nutrition

Regular meals in a relaxed atmosphere. A warm breakfast is considered a good start into the day.

The main meals ought to be taken for lunch – supper in the early evening. Pay attention to feeling hungry or sated: don't eat too much nor remain hungry is the rule

Prepare the meals freshly from natural, regional products. Frozen, heat-conserved, industrially prepared or foodstuffs cooked in the microwave oven are rejected.

Choice of foodstuffs according to the season: more cooling food in summer, more warming food in winter.

Eat cooked food at least twice a day. Food and drinks ought to be lukewarm, never ice-cold or hot.

Raw vegetables, briefly cooked vegetables, freshly squeezed juices and mineral water are not recommended. Milk and dairy products are only included in the diet if they don't cause problems.

Don't use therapeutic recipes over a longer period without consulting your doctor or therapist.

Varied food

Enjoy the diversity of foodstuffs. Characteristics of a balanced nutrition are variety, suitable combination and a balanced quantity of rich and low energy foodstuffs (on one hand avoiding undersupply with essential nutrients and on the other hand to take to many undesirable substances).

A lot of Cereal Products - and Potatoes

Bread, pasta, rice, cereal flakes (best wholemeal) as well as potatoes contain almost no fat, but many vitamins, mineral nutrients, trace elements, roughage and secondary plant substances. These foodstuffs ought to be taken with low-fat side dishes.

Vegetables and Fruit – „Take Five" every day …

5 portions of vegetables and fruit a day, as fresh as possible, briefly cooked, or maybe one portion as a juice – ideal as a side dish to every meal as well as snack between meals: Thus a lot of vitamins, mineral nutrients as well as roughage and secondary plant substances

Daily milk and dairy products
Milk and Dairy Products every Day, once or twice per Week Fish; meat, sausages as well as eggs moderately. These foodstuffs contain valuable nutrients like calcium in the milk, iodine selenium and omega-3 fat acids in saltwater fish. Meat is favorable due to its high content of disposable iron and the vitamins B1, B6 and B12. Quantities of 300 – 600 g meat and sausage per week are sufficient. Prefer low-fat products, especially in meat- and dairy products.

Low-fat and fatty Foodstuffs
Fat supplies us with essential fat acids and fatty foodstuffs contain also fat-soluble vitamins. Fat is high in energy; therefore much fat in the food may cause overweight, possibly also cancer. Too many saturated fat acids may further a tendency for cardio-vascular diseases in the long term. Prefer vegetable oils and fats (e.g. rapeseed-, olive-, soya-oils and solid fats produced therefrom). Beware of invisible fat in meat- and dairy products, pastry and sweets as well as in fast-food and convenience foods. 70 – 90 g fat per day is sufficient.

Moderately Sugar and Salt
Take sugar and foods/drinks containing various kinds of sugar (e.g. glucose syrup) only occasionally. Use herbs and spices as well as a little salt creatively. Prefer salt containing iodine.

Plenty of Liquids
Water is absolutely essential. Drink 1-2 l liquids every day. Prefer water (with or without gas) and other low-calorie drinks. Alcoholic drinks should not be taken.

Tasty Dishes, carefully cooked
Cook the meals with as low temperatures and as short as possible, using little water and fat – this preserves the original taste, keeps the nutrients intact and prevents the production of harmful compounds.

Take time and enjoy the food
Take your Time and enjoy your Food
Eating consciously helps to eat right. The eye enjoys food, too. It's fun, invites to enjoy varied dishes and stimulates the feeling of satiety.

Watch your Weight and stay in Motion
A balanced diet and a lot of exercise and sport (30 – 60 min/day) are a healthy combination. The right weight furthers well-being and health. Thermals, directional effectiveness, digestive power

There are various criteria for judging the effectiveness of herbs and foodstuffs.

The use of certain herbs and ingredients is based on observations of the effects on the body which these foodstuffs, herbs and spices show after having eaten them. The medical science has developed following system: Every ingredient or herb has a directional effectiveness. Furthermore, there are herbs which have a special effect on certain organs.

The basic condition for a healthy metabolism is to obtain sufficient energy from food and that the digestive process doesn't use too much energy. An easily digestible meal makes content and sated, doesn't cause flatulence and fatigue after the meal. The perfect spices increase the healthiness of our meals. Very often, just small doses of herbs and spices will suffice. They are not used to make us sated, but to help our digestive organs to digest the food.

12.2 Recipes

The recipes list the ingredients to be used and the cooking instructions show how the dish is prepared. The list of ingredients shows the concerned quantities as well as the relevance for the therapy. If you find „less than mentioned", try to comply or find an alternative from the „list of recommended foodstuffs". Mostly it shall result just in a small change of taste when you simply avoid this ingredient.

Mild cooking methods: boiling, stewing, poaching, steaming
Strong cooking methods: barbecuing, roasting, frying, smoking
Balanced cooking methods: deep-frying, baking brick
Deep-freezing and warming in the microwave oven should be avoided (denaturalization).

12.3 Foodstuffs

Foodstuffs have an effect on body and soul like medicinal herbs, only a very much milder one. Dietary advice is mainly based on regional foodstuffs. The knowledge about the effects of each foodstuff and the knowledge, when which foodstuff shall be used, is based on the orthodox school of medicine. Use ecologic-organic products, if possible. As everything should be cooked for a long time due to a better digestability and very rarely eaten raw, the food agrees with everyone.

The classification of the foodstuffs according to their effect on the body is the basis in order to achieve a harmonious status of health.

Dietary advisors do not recommend certain foodstuffs for everyone. The individual diet is tailor-made for the individual constitution.

Buy only fresh and ripe fruit and vegetables. You ought to leave unripe fruit and vegetables and such with brown spots and wilted leaves behind in the market. In this case take deep-frozen goods (never ready-to-serve dishes!). Fruit and vegetables are deep-frozen immediately after harvesting and often contain more vitamins and minerals than the goods from the vegetable shelf. Whereas conserved or tinned goods contain very much less biological substances. Also, salt, sugar and others are mostly added to the latter. Never leave the foodstuffs in the water after washing them to avoid that many vital substances get drowned. Clean salads, fruit and vegetables immediately before serving.

Please make sure of the hygienic processing of foodstuffs. Clean your salads, fruit and vegetables carefully. When cooking with meat, prepare all ingredients first and then process the meat products. Clean the worktop and tools very carefully. Wooden surfaces ought to be treated with a mild disinfectant regularly in order to reduce germination.

Store fruit and vegetables separately, if possible. Harvested fruit and vegetables are still alive and emit e.g. ethylene gas, which makes other products ripen and age faster. Keep meat and fish in the closed packaging or store them in the fridge in closed containers.

12.4 Herbs

There are some basic rules for storing medicinal herbs. On principle, herbs must be protected from direct sunlight, humidity and heat.

Containers for the storage of herbs may be glasses, ceramic jars and even plastic containers. However, plastic is a rather unsuitable material and should only be a short-term solution. In case of glass containers, use a dark material.

Medicinal herbs cannot be kept for any long period. The shelf life of herbs is limited. However, it can be prolonged with suitable storage. The place should be dark, rather cool and absolutely dry. A wooden medicine cabinet, placed not directly next to a source of heat, would be ideal. Never buy large quantities of herbs so as not to have to throw them away. Label the container with the name of the herb and the date of harvesting or processing.

13 Other dietic-books

The following syndromes of dietetics, TCM or for a therapy supplement for cancer are available.

Dietetics

E001. Nutrition of the infant - baby food
E002. Nutrition during lactation
E003. Nutrition in old age
E004. Nutrition of children and adolescents
E005. Nutrition of athletes
E006. Light weight
E007. Pregnancy
E008. Full food

Protein and electrolyte - kidneys
E009. (hemodialysis) dialysis treatment
E010. Acute renal failure
E011. Chronic renal insufficiency
E012. Nephrotic syndrome
E013. Kidney stones (nephrolithiasis)

Gastrointestinal tract - pancreas
E014. Acute pancreatitis (inflammation of the pancreas)
E015. Chronic pancreatitis (inflammation of the pancreas)

Gastrointestinal tract - small intestine and large intestine
E016. Acute obstipation (constipation)
E017. Chronic obstipation (constipation)
E018. Colon irritabile
E019. Diverticulitis
E020. Acquired lactose intolerance (lactose malabsorption)
E021. Fructose malabsorption
E022. Glutensensitive enteropathy (celiac disease)
E023. Colectomy
E024. Short Bowel Syndrome

Gastrointestinal tract - liver, gallbladder, bile ducts
E025. Acute and chronic hepatitis (inflammation of the liver)
E026. Cholelithiasis (bile stones)
E027. fatty liver
E028. cirrhosis

Gastrointestinal tract - Stomach and duodenal intestine
E029. Acute gastritis
E030. Chronic gastritis
E031. Stomach bleeding
E032. Ulcus ventriculi and duodenal ulcer
E033. Condition after gastric surgery

Gastrointestinal tract - oral cavity and esophagus
E034. Stomatitis
E035. Esophageal carcinoma (esophageal cancer)
E036. Refluosophagitis (heartburn)

Special diseases
E037. Phenylketonuria (PKU)
E038. Rheumatic joint diseases

Metabolism
E039. Obesity (overweight)
E040. Diabetes mellitus
E041. Eating disorders (underweight)

Fat metabolism
E042. Hypercholesterolaemia (increased cholesterol level)
E043. Hepatic Encephalopathy

Heart and circulation
E044. Arteriosclerosis (arterial calcification)
E045. Heart insufficiency
E046. Hypertension
E047. Hyperuricaemia and gout

Changed nutrient requirements
E048. In case of fever
E049. For malignant diseases
E050. After burns
E051. Radiation and chemotherapy

CANCER
E100. Pancreatic cancer
E101. Bladder cancer
E102. Blood cancer (leukemia)
E103. Breast cancer
E104. Colorectal cancer
E105. Gastric cancer
E106. Kidney cancer
E107. Esophageal cancer

TCM
E200. Bladder - moisture heat in the bladder
E201. Bladder - moisture and cold in the bladder
E202. Bladder - emptiness and cold in the bladder
E203. Large intestine - external cold affects the large intestine
E204. Large intestine - moisture heat in the large intestine
E205. Large intestine - heat blocks the intestine II acute
E206. Large intestine - dryness of the colon
E207. Large intestine - Yang deficiency (cold)
E208. Heart - Blood insufficiency
E209. Heart - Blood stagnation
E210. Heart - Fire
E211. Heart - Hot mucus clogs the heart pores

E212. Heart - Cold mucus clogs the heart pores
E213. Heart - Qi deficiency
E214. Heart - Yang deficiency
E215. Heart - Yin deficiency
E216. Liver - Ascending Liver Yang
E217. Liver - Blood deficiency
E218. Liver - Blood stagnation
E219. Liver - Moisture heat in liver and gall bladder
E220. Liver - Fire
E221. Liver - Gall bladder Qi-Empty
E222. Liver - Cold in the liver meridian
E223. Liver - Qi stagnation
E224. Liver - Wind
E225. Liver - Wind with ascending liver Yang
E226. Liver - Wind with blood anemic
E227. Liver - Wind with extreme heat
E228. Lung - Qi deficiency
E229. Lung - Mucus-moisture in the lungs
E230. Lung - Mucus-heat in the lungs
E231. Lung - Mucus-cold in the lungs
E232. Lung - Dryness of the lungs
E233. Lung - Wind-heat attacks the lungs
E234. Lung - Wind-cold affects the lungs
E235. Lung - Yin deficiency
E236. Stomach - Bloodstagnation
E237. Stomach - Fire
E238. Stomach - Cold with liquid
E239. Stomach - Nutrition stagnation
E240. Stomach - Qi deficiency
E241. Stomach - Rebellious Qi
E242. Stomach - Yin Emptiness
E243. Spleen - Heat and moisture attack the spleen
E244. Spleen - Coldness and moisture affects the spleen
E245. Spleen - Qi deficiency
E246. Spleen - Qi deficiency + Declining spleen Qi
E247. Spleen - Qi deficiency + spleen does not control the blood
E248. Spleen - Yang deficiency
E249. Kidney - Heart and kidney no longer communicate
E250. Kidney - Jing deficiency
E251. Kidney - Kidneys cannot receive the Qi
E252. Kidney - Qi is not stable
E253. Kidney - Yang deficiency
E254. Kidney - Yin deficiency

For further information visit di-book.com.

FSC

www.fsc.org

MIX

Papier aus ver-
antwortungsvollen
Quellen
Paper from
responsible sources

FSC® C105338